PROJECT ★Citizen

A PORTFOLIO-BASED CIVIC EDUCATION PROGRAM

TEACHER'S GUIDE
LEVEL 1

Administered by the Center for Civic Education
in cooperation with the National Conference of State Legislatures

We the People: Project Citizen
is directed by the Center for Civic Education
and funded by the U.S. Department of Education under the
Education for Democracy Act approved by the United States Congress.

FOR ADDITIONAL INFORMATION, PLEASE CONTACT

Project Citizen
Center for Civic Education
5145 Douglas Fir Road, Calabasas, CA 91302-1440
818.591.9321 FAX 818.591.9330
www.civiced.org

Project Citizen
National Conference of State Legislatures
7700 East First Place, Denver, CO 80230-7143
303.364.7700 FAX 303.364.7800
www.ncsl.org

© 2009 Center for Civic Education
11 10 09   01 02 03

ISBN 10   0-89818-236-0
ISBN 13   978-0-89818-236-1

ACKNOWLEDGMENTS

Project Citizen Program Director
Michael Fischer

Curriculum Developers
Charles N. Quigley
Margaret S. Branson
Roy Erickson
Duane E. Smith

Editorial Director
Mark Gage

Editor
David Hargrove

Creative Director
Mark Stritzel

Design
Mark Stritzel
Erin Breese

Contributing Teachers
Sally Broughton, Bozeman, Montana
Deirdre G. Fauntleroy, Burbank, California
Carol V. Paola, Gulfport, Mississippi
Monique Taylor, Aurora, Colorado
Jackie Viana, Hialeah, Florida

A NOTE TO READERS

Dear Students, Teachers, and Parents:

We at the Center for Civic Education welcome your participation in We the People: Project Citizen, a program in civic education. We hope you will find it interesting and worthwhile.

In the words of Abraham Lincoln, we have inherited a government that is "of the people, by the people, and for the people." Our right to participate in governing ourselves in order to protect our rights and promote our common welfare carries certain responsibilities. Among these responsibilities are the need to develop the knowledge and skills to participate intelligently and the willingness to promote liberty and justice for all people.

We believe this program will add to students' knowledge, enhance their skills, and deepen their understanding of how we can all work together to make our communities better.

We wish you well, and we hope that you find the program a stimulating and valuable experience.

Sincerely,

Charles N. Quigley
Executive Director

CONTENTS

INTRODUCTION

PURPOSE

The vibrancy and stability of a democratic society can be gauged, in part, by the degree to which its citizens participate in the civic affairs of the community. As citizens in a representative democracy, we not only have the right, but also the responsibility, to participate in our own governance at every level — from school and neighborhood to state and nation. Project Citizen is designed to assist young people in understanding not only how to participate effectively, but also why they should participate. Project Citizen is a valuable instructional tool whose primary purpose is to prepare a new generation of citizens to be competent, confident, and committed to civic participation.

GOALS

Project Citizen introduces students to and educates them in the methods and procedures used in our governmental processes. The goal of the program is to develop students' commitment to active citizenship and governance by

- Providing the knowledge and teaching the skills required for effective participation
- Providing practical experience designed to foster a sense of competence and efficacy
- Developing an understanding of the importance of citizen participation

We believe this program will add to students' knowledge, enhance their skills, and deepen their understanding of how we can work together to improve our communities.

INTRODUCING PROJECT CITIZEN TO THE CLASS

Begin by having students read and discuss the **Introduction** on pages 1–3 of the student book. Provide an overview of the instructional program and the showcase events. Review with students the information in the **Introduction**, which provides an overview of tasks to be completed for the project. Refer to the **Problem/Solution** illustration on page vi of the student text to help students understand the steps they will be taking.

If students will be participating in a showcase event, it is important that you point out that the showcase is *not* a competition. It is an opportunity for them to publicly display their work in a class portfolio and present it in a simulated public hearing along with the other participating classes. It is most important that students concentrate on doing their best while learning the process. The knowledge and skills they gain and the attitudes they develop toward civic participation will endure far beyond the end of the showcase event.

PUBLIC POLICY

PURPOSE

Helping students develop an understanding of the concept of public policy and the policymaking process is a prerequisite to successful attainment of the goals and purposes of the Project Citizen instructional program. It is recommended that the teacher work with students to develop an understanding of the concept of public policy and the policymaking process as they are generally understood and used by political scientists.

A CLASS DISCUSSION

Defining public policy

This program focuses on the development of a public policy to deal with a specific problem in the community, and if the teacher and class decide to do so, the recommendation of that policy to the appropriate governing body or governmental agency. It is necessary, therefore, that students understand the term "public policy."

As used in this program, a public policy is an agreed-upon way that our government, at whatever level, fulfills its responsibilities, such as protecting the rights of individuals and promoting the welfare of all the people. Typically, public policies are written into laws by legislatures. Other policies, however, are contained in orders, rules, and regulations created by executive branches of government, and in some instances, the decisions of courts at various levels.

Because one of the main goals of this program is to help people learn how to participate in their government, we want students to examine problems that are, or should be, dealt with (at least partially) by government. The solutions students develop to these problems, therefore, should include recommendations as to what policies government should be responsible for implementing. The policies suggested also may include recommendations regarding the shared responsibilities of the people in a community.

B ACTIVITY

Using newspapers to introduce public policy

- **Time required**   Two standard class periods
- **Materials needed**   Several copies of the local newspaper (8 to 12 copies per class or group) and a copy of Student Handouts 1 and 2 for each student.

First Class Period

1   Distribute Student Handout 1: "What Is Public Policy?" (Appendix H, page 89) and ask students to complete the first box with their own ideas about what they think public policy means.

2   Next, ask the entire class the question: "What is public policy?" Using a brainstorming strategy, record all responses on a chalk-board, overhead, or chart paper. Leave these posted for use in the next step.

3   Divide the class into smaller groups of three or four students each. Distribute one complete copy of the local newspaper (include all sections) to each small group. Each group should select four or five articles that reflect its understanding of what public policy is. Each article chosen must come from a different section of the newspaper (for example, national or state news, business, or sports). Groups should be prepared to present and defend each selected article as an example of public policy.

4   Call on each group to present one of its choices and defend the choice as an example of public policy before the class. Groups that follow should not use an article from a section of the newspaper used by any previous group.

5   Use the examples that students gave to conduct a discussion of what the essential elements of public policy are. Have students record this information in the second box of the "What Is Public Policy?" worksheet. Some typical answers might include, but are not limited to, the following:

- Government action
- Authority
- Common good
- Community input
- Protecting citizens
- Solving a problem

6   Following the class discussion of essential elements of public policy, allow time for the small groups to write a definition of public policy, copy it to chart paper, and then present the definition to the class.

7 After all groups have presented their definition, the teacher should highlight or record all the common terms or phrases that are present in each of the definitions.

8 From these common elements, newspaper examples, and original brainstorming work, the class should develop a consensus definition of public policy.

Optional activity

As a research assignment, ask the students to collect several definitions of public policy from various sources. Have students compare their definitions. Allow time to refine, revise, or rewrite the class definition, if desired.

Second Class Period

1 Distribute Student Handout 2: "What Is and What Is Not Public Policy?" (Appendix H, page 90). Review the directions with students and discuss the examples given for the first problem. Return to the definition students wrote as a class in the first part of the lesson and ask them to explain how it fits the examples.

2 Ask students to generate their own solutions for one or more of the given community problems. Then have students form small groups of three or four to share their individual solutions.

3 Next, assign one of the community problems to each group and have group members reach consensus on one solution that is public policy and one solution that is not. Have each group prepare to present its work to the entire class.

4 To check for understanding, have students generate at least two more problems from their own community to complete the empty boxes on the worksheet. Then, either individually or in class as homework, have the students give possible solutions for each problem.

Debriefing Questions

1 What did you learn about the meaning of public policy?

2 Did your understanding of public policy change as a result of this activity?

3 Who has responsibility for making public policy?

4 How might existing public policy get changed?

C CLASS DISCUSSION

What is and what is not public policy?

Have students read the material on page 6 of the student book. You may use the problems the students identified and discussed in doing Activity B on page 5 of the student text to complete the suggested activity.

Another option is to use Student Handout 2: "What Is and What Is Not Public Policy?" (Appendix H, page 90) as a class activity. Student Handout 2 could also be used as an evaluation instrument to check for understanding of what constitutes public policy and what does not.

Activities for introducing the policymaking process

It is important that students understand the central role of government (local, state, and national) in formulating public policy. They should also understand, however, that government's role is only one part of the process; all citizens in a community should be encouraged to participate as well. Democratic decision making requires both the consent of citizens to be governed and their participation in that government.

Policymaking might begin when people in a community perceive that a problem exists. Perceptions about a problem may emerge from the media, politicians, citizen groups, or institutions of government. Next, people might formulate ideas for how best to resolve the problem. People with ideas try to persuade government to adopt their ideas and put their solutions into practice. In this process, there are likely to be differences of opinion over what should be done about a particular problem and who should do it. Frequently, alternative proposals emerge.

The entire process includes collecting and analyzing data, assessing consequences of alternative actions, and gathering support for one proposal or another. Once people agree on an appropriate course of action, they must persuade the appropriate government or governmental agency to adopt the policy. Once the policy is adopted, it must then be carried out.

POLICYMAKING PROCESS

The flowchart below shows how the policymaking process occurs
in most circumstances. Reviewing the flowchart with the class can help
students gain a clear understanding of this complex process. A reproducible
copy is provided in Student Handout 3: "Policymaking Process Diagram"
(Appendix H, page 91).

POLICYMAKING PROCESS

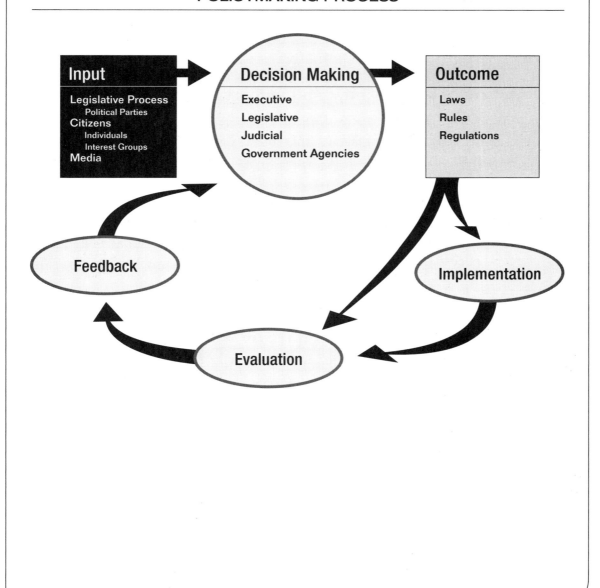

After you have explained the policy flow depicted on the chart, divide the class into small working groups of four students each. Have students discuss the chart and then do some research to develop a better understanding of the process as it applies to their local or state government bodies.

Next, divide the chart into four discrete sectors: (1) Input, (2) Decision Making, (3) Outcomes, and (4) Implementation (including Evaluation and Feedback). Assign, or allow each member of the group to select, one of the four sectors and have each member develop two or three paragraphs that explain that part of the chart. After each person has finished his or her writing task, have the group members edit the four sections into an essay that describes the policymaking process.

D   ACTIVITY

Government officials have the authority to make public policy

One of the important ideas that students will need to learn about public policy is that there are a number of different policymakers who may have the authority and some responsibility for dealing with a problem.

Have students read and discuss the material in the first column on page 7 of the student text. Have them complete **Activity D** on the same page, using the "Government Responsibilities Worksheet" on page 8, as an in-class activity or a homework assignment. Refer to Student Handout 4 (Appendix H, page 92) for a reproducible copy of the worksheet.

E   CLASS DISCUSSION

Citizen participation in the policymaking process

One of the important ideas that students will need to learn about public policy is that there are a number of different policymakers who may have the authority and some responsibility for dealing with a problem.

It is important that students understand the role of citizens in formulating public policies. Citizens can be involved at all levels of the process by attending public meetings, writing letters to their representatives and to newspapers, making phone calls and sending email messages, monitoring proposals and counterproposals, participating in demonstrations, persuading other citizens to support a particular alternative, conducting research, submitting proposals of their own, and giving testimony at public hearings. This is only a partial list, but it illustrates that there are numerous opportunities for citizens to participate in the decision-making process.

Activities for introducing the policymakers

Refer to the sample worksheet, Student Handout 5A: "Who Are the Responsible Policymakers" (Appendix H, page 93), to show students how different policymakers might have responsibility for dealing with the common problem of school truancy. After discussing the example, give students a copy of Student Handout 5B: "Who Are the Responsible Policymakers?" (Appendix H, page 94). Have students work in small groups of three or four. Ask each group to identify a problem in the school or community that is likely to require a public policy solution, develop a chart for the problem they select, and then present their work to the class.

Have students read the material on page 9 of the student text. Identify one or two of the public policy issues in the community that students identified earlier in **Activity B** on page 5. Ask them to give specific examples of how each of the ways to participate might be applied to that problem. Try to get students to be specific about the meetings, officials, newspapers, and public events that might be relevant to the problems being discussed in the activity.

PREPARING YOUR CLASS

Employ the following procedures to prepare your class to participate in Project Citizen.

1 Working with adult volunteers

It is recommended that you ask adults to volunteer to assist students with the tasks necessary to develop the class portfolio. Volunteers may be parents, senior citizens, teacher aides, youth organization leaders, or other civic-minded people. Volunteers might have real-life experience in the application of the ideas under consideration. They can enrich field experiences by serving as guides and responding to questions. They also might establish ongoing relationships in which they make themselves available to respond to questions or issues that arise during the program.

The following Guidelines for Adult Volunteer Assistance is adapted from Appendix A on pages 44–45. Appendix A may be copied and distributed to adult volunteers.

1a Suggestions for utilizing adult volunteers

Assisting with tasks and procedures

Adult volunteers can help students understand the steps they must take in developing their Project Citizen portfolios. Volunteers should review the "Project Citizen Portfolio Criteria Checklist" on page 49 of the student book. They can copy and distribute the "Project Citizen Portfolio Criteria Checklist" (Appendix G, page 85). This will guide students through a self-evaluation.

Gathering information

Volunteers can help students identify sources of information that could be useful to them. They can explain how to gather information about the problem under consideration efficiently and effectively. For example, adult volunteers might help students

- Find information at a library
- Locate and use computers to find information and valuable resources available on the Internet
- Use telephone books or computer-based directories to locate government officials or agencies and appropriate private organizations that may have pertinent information
- Contact people in the community who might serve as good sources of information

- Write letters or emails requesting information
- Prepare to interview resource individuals by role-playing that person
- Provide transportation to interviews and other places where students can gather information

Preparing presentations

Adult volunteers can coach students in creating and organizing oral presentations of their portfolio. They can help set up presentations before community groups or government bodies.

Reflecting on the experience

Volunteers can help students prepare written statements about what they have learned by participating in the Project Citizen program. They can focus students' attention on what knowledge they gained, what civic skills they developed, and how their attitudes and dispositions about their roles as citizens in a representative democracy changed. Volunteers can ask what problems they encountered and what they would do differently if they were to develop another portfolio.

1b   Limiting the assistance of adult volunteers

Gathering information

Adults should not assist students by

- Collecting information for them
- Writing letters and emails or making phone calls for them
- Doing research that students should perform on their own

Portfolio preparation

Adults should not assist students by

- Writing materials for them to include in the portfolio
- Preparing their presentation statements
- Creating illustrations or other graphics
- Selecting materials to include in the portfolio

Oral presentation preparation

Adults should not prepare presentations for students.
See Appendix A on pages 44–45.

2 Holding public showcase events

Guidelines and Procedures for Conducting a Showcase Event are included as Appendix B on pages 46–50 of this guide.

3 Evaluating the portfolio and simulated public hearing

Materials to help you organize and conduct showcase events in your classroom or another public venue are provided in Appendix B on pages 46–50.

Guidelines for the community members you select to serve as evaluators are provided in Appendix C (pages 51–56) and Appendix E (pages 59–64).

Rating sheets for use by evaluators in assessing student achievement in the portfolio and hearing can be found in Appendix D (pages 57–58) and Appendix F (pages 65–66). These rating sheets may also be used by teachers as tools for assessing student work and performance, whether or not a showcase is held.

HELPING YOUR STUDENTS TO DEVELOP THEIR PORTFOLIO FOR A SIMULATED HEARING

Help your students understand the steps involved in selecting a problem for study, developing their portfolio, and preparing for a simulated public hearing by using these suggestions. Feel free to change or modify these steps in any way you think might be more useful for your class. We have asked experienced Project Citizen teachers to provide us with some of their best ideas and suggestions based on their own trial and error. These **Teaching Tips** are included at the end of each step. We hope you find these ideas helpful in making Project Citizen a successful educational experience for your students.

STEP 1

IDENTIFYING PUBLIC POLICY PROBLEMS IN YOUR COMMUNITY

PURPOSE

Discuss the purpose with students. The purpose of **Step 1** is to have students

- Become aware of what they already know about problems in their community

- Discuss these problems with their parents, neighbors, or other members of the community to find out what they know and what they think about these problems

- Gather enough information to select a problem that the class agrees is important to study

A   CLASS DISCUSSION

Discuss what students know about problems in communities

A list of problems common to many communities is provided on pages 10–11 of the student book to focus attention on this task. These problems should be presented as a springboard to generate student thinking about issues in their own community. Inform your students that they are not expected to select one of the problems mentioned in the book for their own project. Instead, they may select another problem that is more significant to their community.

If you conducted the activity on pages 4–5 of this guide, "Using Newspapers to Introduce Public Policy," the students may have already identified relevant issues in their community to further investigate.

B   SMALL GROUP ACTIVITY

It is important for the class to select a problem for which they can propose a reasonable and workable public policy, one that necessitates government involvement at some level, and to some extent, in its solution.

Lead students in an initial discussion of what they already know about the problems listed in the student text. Then ask them to brainstorm other problems they are aware of in their community. After they are satisfied with their list of problems (those given in the text or their own), divide the class into groups of two or three students and assign one problem to each group. Each group should complete the small group activity described on page 11 of the student book, using the "Problem Identification and Analysis Form" on page 12 to record their answers. Finally, have students report and discuss their responses.

C HOMEWORK ASSIGNMENTS

Assign homework

Assign the homework described on page 13. You may divide the class into groups, each responsible for one or more of the three assignments, depending on their interests and abilities. Make sure students know how to use the forms provided in the student book on pages 14–16. The work that students do in this step will be used in Step 2.

NOTE Students may use the forms in their books or you may reproduce them for their use. A reproducible set of these forms is provided in this guide as Appendix G, Forms 1–14 (pages 67–87).

D REFLECTION

Although Step 6 – "Reflecting on Your Learning Experience" deals with an overall reflection on the entire Project Citizen process, it is important to conduct a reflection activity at the end of each step. This reflection should deal with the specific purpose and activities in that step. Some sample questions for reflection on Step 1 include the following:

1   What are the best ways for people to learn about the problems in their community?

2   What did you learn about problems your community faces?

3   Does everyone have a responsibility to know and understand the problems in their community? Why or why not?

4   Is it the responsibility of government to deal with every problem the community has? Why or why not?

5   What can happen to a community if citizens ignore its problems?

Experienced teachers who have successfully taught Project Citizen to their classes shared the ideas and suggestions that follow.

1 At the beginning of the year, put up an "Interest Board." Each time students find a problem of interest, they can place it on the Interest Board. When the class starts Step 1 – "Identifying Public Policy Problems in Your Community," revisit the Interest Board to review the problems posted there as possible topics to research. Students will find that some of the topics have been solved or are no longer of interest, whereas other problems have grown in intensity.

2 To get students thinking about the problem selection process, have the class scan newspapers throughout the year for current events and public policy issues that deal with the school, the local community, and the state.

3 As an out-of-class assignment, have students interview various members of the community for ideas about issues or problems they see. For example, they might interview someone younger than themselves, then someone older than their parents. The issues and problems generated from the interviews can be added to the list.

Make this a literacy lesson by having students write an essay on what they learned about their community from the interviews they conducted. These essays will also help the students clarify the ideas presented.

4 Invite your principal or school district superintendent to talk about problems he or she has encountered in the school or school district. Share the list of problems brainstormed by the class and encourage students to discuss their concerns with the administrator. This allows administrators an opportunity to be involved in the project from the beginning and support it as the students progress.

5 Invite a local city or town official to the classroom to discuss problems in the community. Other possible guests might be heads of commissions or leaders of community organizations. Special interest groups can also provide useful information.

6 Invite a state senator or representative to the classroom to discuss the problems that interest her or him for legislative action. The National Conference of State Legislatures is a partner in Project Citizen and offers an exciting program called America's Legislators Back to School. Learn more about this program by visiting http://www.ncsl.org/public/backsch.htm

7 When your students choose their Project Citizen problem, make sure it has been narrowed down to manageable dimensions. One strategy is to use a tree diagram. For example, students might identify world hunger as a problem. World hunger could become the trunk of the tree. In the tree's branches, students can identify related problems that are not as broad in scope. For example, students coming to school hungry, starving people on the streets of their community, etc.

8 Make sure the problems students come up with are public policy issues. This way, when they get to Step 2 – "Selecting a Problem for Class Study," they will be choosing from an established pool of problems that already reflect public policy issues.

Also, make sure the problems that students come up with are stated as such. For example, "school resources" does not state a problem. A better statement would be "Our school does not have enough computers."

9 Always try to involve other faculty and staff in the project. Social studies, language arts, math, and science teachers can play a major role in making the project a success. Also, the school librarian or media specialist, art teacher, computer or technology teacher, and other staff members can be helpful in the successful completion of the project.

STEP 2

PURPOSE

Discuss the purpose with students. The purpose of **Step 2** is to have students

- Identify what the class has learned about problems in their community
- Decide if they need more information before selecting a problem
- Select one problem for the class to study

A   CLASS DISCUSSION

Examine information gathered

Your class should examine what they have learned about community problems before selecting the single problem they will study as a class. We suggest you use the procedures that follow to lead a discussion about what students learned from their work in Step 1.

Discuss questions such as these:

1   What have you learned about community problems from the people you interviewed?

2   Which of the problems seem to be most significant?

3   Are these problems that can be solved by developing public policies?

4   Which appear to be problems for which existing public policies need to be changed?

5   Which community problems are of greatest significance and concern to you?

Your students will have learned that every community faces problems. Some of the problems they considered may apply only to their own community, whereas others are much larger and can be found in most communities. Finding a problem topic that your students are interested in and making sure that it is something they can handle successfully is not always easy.

For example, we know that not everyone in the world has enough food to eat. Individuals and whole families throughout the world are faced with long- and short-term food shortages due to bad weather, war, poverty, and other causes. Taking on the problem of world hunger for the project is too big a task and the students are not likely to be able to conduct successful research and reach viable solutions in the form of public policy. If students are really interested in taking on the topic of hunger, you could move them toward a problem of individuals or groups in their own community who do not have adequate food, such as the homeless, the working poor, the elderly, or children who come to school without adequate nutrition.

Consider these guidelines, which the class can use when they weigh the possible problems for study:

1 Does government have the authority and responsibility
   to create a policy to deal with this problem?

2 Is it reasonable to believe that a public policy should
   be written to resolve the problem?

3 Can the problem be handled with a public policy
   that is both practical and realistic?

4 If the problem is really important to your community,
   does it have some impact on you?

5 Will you be able to find enough information to develop
   a complete and persuasive portfolio?

If some of the problems listed do not meet these guidelines, you may encourage your students to eliminate them from consideration. Once the class has a short list of problems that do meet these guidelines, you will need to work with the students to reach consensus on the one problem they will all study.

Reach a class consensus on a problem to study

When the students think they are ready, have them reach consensus on a problem for class study. Although conducting a simple majority vote is one way to do this, it may not always be conducive to successful completion of the project. An important goal of Project Citizen is to help students learn that in a democracy, it is not always possible to get everything they want. Learning that negotiation and compromise are vital parts of the policymaking process is underscored by conducting an open, deliberative process where each student has a chance to express his or her view and have his or her concerns aired. If well conducted, this consensus-building process can help move those students who are not interested in or are reluctant to undertake a particular problem to see its significance and convince them to join willingly with the others to work on the problem.

Because everyone in the class will be working on the same problem, it is important that all students reach some level of agreement about the problem to ensure that all students are willing to participate. Reaching a group consensus means several things. First, it means that everyone has had a chance to express his or her ideas freely. It also means that there has been a sharing of different opinions and different points of view about the problems being considered. No student should feel forced to make a choice he or she did not want because of pressure from other students or the teacher. Finally, there should be some effort to combine the different ideas and opinions into the final agreement.

You can do the Small Group Activity below with your class to help them better internalize the concept and practice of consensus and consensus building.

B SMALL GROUP ACTIVITY

What does it mean to reach consensus?

Consensus does not necessarily mean that there is one hundred percent agreement. But what does it mean? Divide the class into small groups of two or three students. Have them undertake the following activities and share their work in a class discussion.

1   Use a dictionary to look up these terms: consensus, majority, majority rule, and minority rights. Review and discuss the definitions.

2   Next, using their own words, have students write new definitions for each term with an example for each one.

3   Suppose your class had narrowed the problems they wanted to study to these two: (1) improving the school lunch program and (2) building a new skateboard facility in the town park. The teacher calls for a vote and the final result is 15 for the skateboard facility and 14 for the school lunch program. The teacher then announces that the class will study the skateboard issue.

Ask students to answer the following questions individually and then share their answers with the class.

a   If you had wanted to improve school lunches, how would you feel and why?

b   Does majority rule always mean consensus? Why or why not?

c   Why do you think it is important for the class to try to reach consensus on the problem they will study?

Conduct further research, if necessary

If the students do not know enough to make a decision about the problem they want to study, if the discussion leads them to want to explore other problems, or if they cannot reach consensus on the problems they have selected, then assign them to gather information on other problems. Have them use the forms provided in Step 1 of the student book to gather and record information about additional problems.

Significance of the problem selected

The problem selected by the students should be one they chose freely and consider to be important in its impact on a specific group in a given community (e.g., all homeowners on the west side of town or all seventh-graders in a local middle school). The completed portfolio should not be evaluated on the basis of whether the teacher or evaluator necessarily considers the problem chosen for study to be significant or important. Evaluation should be based on how well he class gathers, reports, and evaluates information on the problem and how well they research and develop their proposed public policy, as well as their action plan to promote it.

C REFLECTION

As previously stated, Step 6 – "Reflecting on Your Learning Experience" deals with overall reflection on the Project Citizen process; however, it is important to conduct a reflection activity at the end of each step. This reflection should focus on the specific purpose and activities in that step. Some sample questions for reflection on Step 2 include the following:

1   Was it difficult for your class to reach an agreement on the problem they wanted to study? Why or why not?

2   What made it easy or difficult to decide on the problem to study?

3   Do you feel you had a chance to have your ideas and opinions heard? Why or why not?

4   Why is consensus building an important part of group decision making?

5   What alternatives do you have when the decision the group makes is not the decision you preferred?

TEACHING TIPS

Experienced teachers who have successfully taught Project Citizen to their classes shared the ideas and suggestions that follow.

1 Have students give short presentations explaining what they have found about the issue or problem they analyzed. Allow other students to ask them questions regarding that problem.

Before beginning the presentations, brainstorm possible broad questions the class may want to ask the student presenter. For example, a student may ask, "Is the government involved in solving this problem?" or "What government agency is involved in solving this problem?" Students may ask for clarification of specific ideas related to the problem being presented. Students also may ask if this is a problem that can realistically be solved with a relatively simple policy.

2 Encourage students to prepare an "impassioned plea" for the problem about which they feel most strongly. Sometimes this plea moves other students to recognize the importance of an idea suggested by someone else or conversely shows a student that his or her own suggestion is difficult to defend.

3 Having the class reach consensus on which problem to choose is much more involved than taking a vote in which majority rules. To make sure all students feel they have a chance to be heard, post the problems on the board or on large chart paper. Be sure to eliminate the problems that do not involve a public policy. Then conduct one or more of these consensus-building activities:

• Give each student three colored stickers. Have students place their stickers next to the problem or problems they feel most strongly about. They may put one or more stickers next to a particular problem or problems to indicate how strongly they feel about it. This process helps narrow the initial list and gives good visual feedback about what most interests the class. You can repeat this step to select the problem or narrow the list further.

- Write each of the identified problems on a piece of construction paper and post them in a row along a wall. Have students line up under the problem they feel is the most important. Students then, in turn, explain why they feel this is the most relevant issue to study. After all information has been presented, students may move to another line if they change their minds about the importance of the problem.

- Have students write the problem they feel is most important on a slip of paper. Place these slips in a basket, mix them up, and have students draw a slip at random. Go around the room and have students explain why they think a person would have chosen this problem. See if this information has changed the minds of any students.

4 If, after the problem has been chosen, a few students still do not like the selection, ask them some probing questions such as, "Is there any area of interest that is part of this problem that you would like to explore?" Providing a reluctant student with a specific task within the selected problem may produce some "buy-in" for that student.

5 Every class is likely to have one or two students who are not completely satisfied with the problem the class has chosen. Let these students know that the class needs to research opposing viewpoints to make their project well-rounded and this would be a great task for them to take on.

6 As the teacher, you may feel that the problem the class has selected is not the most pressing public policy issue facing the school or community. If you can ascertain, however, that it is a public policy issue and the students are passionate and committed to using their Project Citizen time to solve it, then you should support their choice. Remember, this is their project, and their problem need not be yours.

7 If you have reservations about taking on a controversial issue or problem that might be opposed or not supported by parents, your administration, or colleagues, you may have to consider not doing the project. You have the right, and in some cases an obligation, not to put yourself or your students at unnecessary risk.

STEP 3

PURPOSE

Discuss the purpose with students. The purpose of **Step 3** is to have students

- Decide where they can get additional information about the problem they have selected

- Recognize that there are a variety of sources that they can use to get needed information

- Learn to evaluate the quality of the sources of information they gather

A CLASS DISCUSSION

Identify sources of information

Once the class has selected a problem, students will need to gather detailed information to use in the development of their portfolio. Lead students in a discussion of the sources of information contained on pages 18–20 of the student book. Add other sources that may be available in your community. As you discuss each potential source, ask students to share what they already know about the source and any experiences with it they might have had. You also might ask students if they know adults affiliated with the source who can be contacted for information. For example, do they know a lawyer, a scholar, a person working in an agency of local government, or a community volunteer? If so, record this information for use by the research teams.

B GUIDELINES

Before asking students to contact sources of information, it is very important to review the guidelines on page 21 of the student book. Be sure that only one student contacts each office to ask for information or make an appointment for an interview so that your assignment does not place too great a burden on busy offices, businesses, or individuals.

C HOMEWORK ASSIGNMENT

Identify the sources of information your class will explore. Then divide the class into research teams, each assigned to obtain information from one type of source. The homework assignment on pages 22–27 of the student text provides guidance for students and the forms to be used to obtain and document information. Review the forms with students, and make sure they understand the questions and how to record responses. One or more adult volunteers may be asked to assist each research team to complete its tasks. Adult volunteers may help the students, but they should not do the students' work for them (see Appendix A on pages 44–45).

D REFLECTION

As previously stated, Step 6 – "Reflecting on Your Learning Experience" deals with overall reflection on the Project Citizen process; however, it is important to conduct a reflection activity at the end of each step. This reflection should focus on the specific purpose and activities in that step. Some sample questions for reflection on Step 3 include the following:

1   What problems did you encounter when you tried to gather information for your project?

2   Were you able to work successfully with your team members to get the information you needed for the project? Why or why not?

3   How did you improve your research skills by gathering information for your project?

4   What were you able to learn about the role of government and government officials when you did the research for your project?

5   Did your opinions about government officials change as a result of doing the research for your project? If they did change, explain in what ways. If not, explain why.

TEACHING TIPS

Experienced teachers who have successfully taught Project Citizen to their classes shared the ideas and suggestions that follow.

1 After the class has successfully completed Step 2 of the project, write "The problem is..." on the board, an overhead, or chart paper. Have the entire class write a few sentences defining the problem so that everyone has the same understanding.

Next, have the class brainstorm the type of information they will want to gather and the sources and methods they might use to find out more about the problem. For example, they might say, "survey all the fifth- through eighth-graders about the lunch menu" or "count the number of cars that pass the school crossing each morning before school begins" or "find magazine articles and health reports about the effects of secondhand smoke on children."

2 Consider using the eight different "Examples of sources of information" found on pages 18–20 of the student book. Use them to help organize research task groups. Use the forms in Appendix G of this guide (pages 72–76) and in the student book on pages 23–27 to help organize the types of research that each "source of information" task group will conduct.

Some research tasks that students are most likely to need include conducting and then summarizing key information from interviews; locating, reading, and writing a summary of relevant documents; creating graphs or charts showing survey results; and collecting photos and drawings relevant to the problem.

The students in each task group should pick a team captain to write each person's name under the task for which they are responsible. The team captain regularly checks the progress of each person in the group.

3 Collecting information from a variety of print and electronic sources is an important part of Step 3. These sources may include books, newspapers, periodicals, brochures, studies, reports, students' own surveys, and the Internet.

- Have students make photocopies or printouts of the documents they find. As they read the material, have them use a highlighter to mark the significant facts and information. Students should prepare a brief summary of the information that is most relevant. Then clip the written summary to the complete document and place it in an appropriate file.

- To be sure that all sources are properly documented, develop a form that specifies what information will be needed for the list of sources, or bibliography. In each research task group, identify one student to be the "bibliography manager" with responsibility for compiling the reference citations and information that will be used later for the portfolio display panels and documentation binder.

- It is important for the students to understand that the way they write survey questions will determine whether the results can be tallied in a meaningful way. Use the problem the class is researching to develop several examples of poorly written survey items so students can see how these might make it difficult to gather the information they need.

- Do not assume that your students' access to and familiarity with newspapers, libraries, and computers is universal. Some students have never performed an Internet search, received an email, visited the local public library, or read a newspaper. Even if they have a computer at home, they may never have used it for academic purposes. If these are relevant issues for your students, you may consider doing much of the research during class time.

4 In addition to print and electronic resources, students are expected to conduct interviews with members of the community to gather additional information and differing points of view. These interviews can be conducted in person, on the phone, or through written communications (letters and email).

- Have students prepare all interview questions ahead of time. Review the questions with students and have them edit the questions as needed.

- Before students begin interviewing community members, they should be given an opportunity to practice interviewing skills. Have two students work together. Ask them to pick a topic and role-play an interview in which one student asks questions and the other responds. Afterward, discuss what the students did well and where they need to improve. You should also practice appropriate ways for students to handle rudeness or not being taken seriously in the interview process.

- Before the students begin to conduct interviews with community members, make every effort to contact people to be interviewed. Inform them about Project Citizen and tell them that a student will be calling them. This will help guarantee a positive interview experience both for students and interviewees.

- If the interviews will be with school staff, email those involved to let them know that the students will be conducting interviews and the topic to be discussed.

- Interviews should be conducted by a team of three students. If possible, use a speakerphone. One student will be responsible for asking the prepared questions and the other two for writing the responses. If there is no speakerphone available, the student conducting the interview should repeat the respondent's answers.

STEP 4

DEVELOPING A CLASS PORTFOLIO

PURPOSE

Discuss the purpose with students. The purpose of **Step 4** is to have students

- Answer important questions as a class that will guide the development of the portfolio
- Divide into four portfolio task groups to complete the development of each of the four parts of the portfolio
- Select and use the best material gathered to complete the four parts of the portfolio

A   CLASS DISCUSSION

Reach a common understanding and agreement with the entire class

At this point, your class should have enough information to begin developing its portfolio. However, experience tells us that it is important to form the four portfolio groups *after* you have completed the procedure described below. If you create the four groups prematurely, students will focus on planning and working on the one set of portfolio tasks they have been assigned rather than giving full attention to each of the four parts of the portfolio. This could result in confusion among the students and a lack of cohesiveness to the final product. From a classroom management perspective, starting the development of the portfolio without this step can also cause Portfolio Groups 3 and 4 to sit idly while Groups 1 and 2 complete their work. Then Groups 1 and 2 will be idle while 3 and 4 finish their work. Therefore, *we strongly recommend* that you use the procedure outlined below to achieve the greatest success.

In a class discussion, have the entire group contribute to developing answers to the questions in the four task worksheets on pages 29–34 of the student book. Masters for copies of Student Handouts 8–11 also appear in Appendix G of this guide (pages 77–82). You may want to begin this task by having students work individually and then compare, discuss, and defend their answers in a class discussion.

Note that one of the more difficult tasks for students will be drafting the language of the proposed public policy. Although the worksheet "Task Three: Proposing a Public Policy" in the student book gives some guidance, it may not be enough. Student

Handout 6: "Proposing a Public Policy" (Appendix H, page 95) provides guidelines to help students understand what is necessary when drafting language for a bill or public policy.

Once all students working together have satisfactorily completed the four task worksheets, you may form the four portfolio groups.

B GROUP TASKS

Divide the class into portfolio groups

Review and discuss with the class the four portfolio group tasks explained on page 35 of the student book. Using your best professional judgment, either allow the students to select the portfolio group task they want to work on or divide the class into the four portfolio groups yourself. Each of the four groups should have a relatively equal number of students.

Review the tasks and specifications for the portfolio

Be sure students in each group understand everything they will be expected to produce. Lead each group in a step-by-step reading and discussion of its overall and specific tasks as they are described in the student book.

Use the information gathered by the research teams

Information gathered in Step 3 by the research teams often will be useful for more than one portfolio group. To make sure each group gets the information it needs, you might have each portfolio group take a turn sitting at a table at the front of the class.

   a   The group at the front of the class should read to the class the questions and explanations it is responsible for addressing in its part of the portfolio display section. As each question is read, ask the students in the class to provide the group with relevant information they have gathered for the particular question. Written or printed information that is useful for more than one group can be duplicated and given to each group.

   b   Each portfolio group should then use the information to complete its tasks as specified in the student text.

Develop the portfolio

Begin the process of having each portfolio group develop its part of the class portfolio. Specific instructions for each portfolio group are given in the student book on the following pages:

- Portfolio Group 1: Explaining the problem, pages 38–39

- Portfolio Group 2: Examining alternative policies to deal with the problem, pages 40–41

- Portfolio Group 3, Proposing a public policy to deal with the problem, pages 42–45 (including the "Constitutional Opinion Form")

- Portfolio Group 4, Developing an action plan, pages 46–47

If a portfolio group does not have all the information required to complete the assigned task, teachers, other students, and adult volunteers should help the group learn how to find the information.

A note on portfolios

A portfolio is a purposeful, integrated collection of student work selected according to specified guidelines. These guidelines vary depending on the subject or discipline and the assessment purpose of the portfolio. Portfolios are most often used as a collection of the selected work of an individual student. In the Project Citizen program, however, each portfolio contains the selected work of an entire class working cooperatively to develop a public policy to address a community problem.

C EVALUATION CRITERIA

In evaluating the portfolios, "selected work" is a critical term

Neither the display nor the documentation section of the class portfolio should be an accumulation of everything the students can find on their topic. Rather, the portfolio should contain only those materials that represent the students' best efforts to address the tasks and their best judgment about which of the materials are the most important. Each individual panel and corresponding section in the documentation binder should be viewed as the same work and evaluated holistically, rather than as two distinctly separate parts. The same is true for the complete portfolio: all four panels and the five sections of the documentation binder should be considered as a unified, interrelated whole.

D GROUP INSTRUCTIONS

Refer to pages 38–47 of the student book for specific instructions for each group.

E | SPECIFICATIONS

Specifications for portfolios

The work of all four groups will be featured in a class portfolio. It will have two sections: display and documentation. Please read the specifications carefully.

a   Display section

The display section should be composed of four sheets of poster board, foam-core board, or the equivalent. *Each of the four panels should be no larger than 32 inches wide by 40 inches high.* Each of the four portfolio groups will have one panel to display its work. This four-panel display should be constructed so it can be placed on a table, bulletin board, or on four easels. *Everything on the display panel must be one-dimensional to allow the four sections to be folded flat without damaging the display material.* When placed together for shipping, the four panels should be no larger than 32 inches wide by 40 inches high and no thicker than 2 inches.

Materials displayed may include written statements, lists of sources, charts, graphs, photographs, original artwork, etc.

b   Documentation section

Each of the four groups should select from the materials gathered those that best document or give evidence of its research. These materials should be placed in a three-ring binder no larger than 2 inches thick. Dividers of different colors should be used to separate the four sections. The binder should include an overall table of contents and a table of contents for each section.

The fifth part of the documentation section should contain the materials suggested in Step 6 — "Reflecting on Your Learning Experience." It also should be separated by a divider.

NOTE   The specifications for the portfolio that appear in the student book and above apply to portfolios that will be entered into local, state, and national showcase events. If your class does not intend to participate beyond the school level, you may develop your own guidelines and standards for the final portfolio.

F REFLECTION

As previously stated, Step 6 – "Reflecting on Your Learning Experience" deals with overall reflection on the Project Citizen process; however, it is important to conduct a reflection activity at the end of each step. This reflection should focus on the specific purpose and activities in that step. Some sample questions for reflection on Step 4 include the following:

1. Did the members of your portfolio group share the work responsibilities and cooperate to get them done well and on time? Why or why not?

2. Were you able to work successfully with your portfolio group members to get the work done? Why or why not?

3. Did every member of your portfolio group take responsibility for getting his or her individual work completed well and on time? Why or why not?

4. What are some ways that the work might have been completed more efficiently?

5. Is it better to work on a project as an individual or with a team? Why?

TEACHING TIPS

Experienced teachers who have successfully taught Project Citizen to their classes shared the ideas and suggestions that follow.

1 The entire class should decide on an appropriate title for the portfolio display. They should also agree on a color scheme, font style and size, and other visual elements so that the portfolio and documentation binder will present a unified look.

2 Work with other teachers in your school as you plan for the design of the class portfolio. For example,

- Involve the art teacher by having him or her talk to the students about design elements that will make an eye-catching and effective visual presentation.

- Ask the math teacher to assist students in creating a variety of graphs and charts to present their information.

- Have the computer technology teacher work with students to learn to use various design programs to create effective visual and graphic material.

3 Forming the portfolio groups can be accomplished in a variety of ways. Some teachers will allow students to self-select whereas other teachers prefer to form the groups themselves. Regardless of the method you choose, it is important that the groups be balanced with a good mix of individual strengths and talents (e.g., manager, negotiator, writer, artist, orator, etc.).

4 Have each portfolio group select one student to serve on a layout team. This team approves final placement of all items on the panels and ensures that there is continuity from one panel to the next. All the groups should provide the layout team with a checklist to ensure that all requirements are met, such as correct number of pages for narrative components, captions on pictures, appropriate pictures for each panel, sources, etc.

5 Have the class choose one student to serve as the photo editor. The photo editor is in charge of acquiring all the photos the class thinks they will need to present their problem and policy solution. If possible, provide this student with a school camera or an inexpensive disposable camera. The photo editor takes the pictures the task groups need, or acquires appropriate photos from other sources.

6 Each portfolio group should have a general editor whose role is to make sure all the required elements for the display panel and documentation binder have been developed. The general editor is also responsible for making sure each graph and picture has a caption and that there is a complete list of citations and sources for all material presented.

7 Use clear sheet protectors for all material that goes into the documentation binder. Do not attempt to number the pages until the binder is complete. Instead of putting page numbers on the papers, have a student write the numbers on the sheet protectors with a permanent marker. This makes it easy to insert additional items without changing numbers on the pages. Compile the table of contents for each section after all items have been inserted in the binder.

8 When the portfolio is completed, have students use the "Project Citizen Portfolio Criteria Checklist" on page 49 of the student text (also see Appendix G, page 85), to make sure they have completed all the important details. Have the students in each task group check their own display panel and section of the documentation binder. Then have the groups use the checklist to assess another section of the portfolio.

9 As a final check of student work, have other teachers, parents, students, and administrators review the panels and binder for corrections or changes.

STEP 5

PRESENTING YOUR PORTFOLIO

PURPOSE

Discuss the purpose with students. The purpose of **Step 5** is to have students

- Gain valuable experience in presenting their ideas to others
- Convince others of the value of the policy they are proposing to solve a community problem

A OPENING

Oral presentation

The oral presentation takes the form of a simulated public hearing that models what would typically occur in many public meetings and hearings conducted by local, state, and federal governments, and by government agencies and departments. It is strongly recommended that every class take part in a simulated public hearing. Participation in the simulated hearing provides students with yet another opportunity to learn how they can participate in their government.

The first four minutes will be the opening presentation during which each of the four portfolio groups will present orally the most significant information from its part of the portfolio.

- The presentation should be based on the portfolio display and documentation section, but should not be a word-for-word reading from the display.

- Use graphics from the portfolio to help explain or emphasize a point.

- Only materials included in the portfolio may be used during the oral presentation. Students may not introduce additional materials such as videotapes, slides, computer demonstrations, etc.

- After the opening statement is made, the evaluators will immediately begin with follow-up questions for that group.

B FOLLOW-UP QUESTIONS

The next six minutes will be spent on follow-up questions during which the panel of evaluators will ask each group about its portfolio presentation. During this time, the evaluators might ask the students to

- Explain further or clarify points they have made

- Give examples of specific points they have made

- Defend some of their statements or positions

- Answer questions about what they learned from their experience: What problems did they have? What were the most important things they learned as they studied this community problem?

C PREPARATION

In the simulation, each of the four portfolio groups presents its prepared statement before a panel of evaluators and then responds to follow-up questions about its section of the portfolio. To prepare students for the oral presentation in public showcases, give them an opportunity to practice before another class or a group of teachers or parents in their own classroom.

D GUIDELINES

This culminating hearing activity is an excellent model for performance-based assessment. Specific instructions for the simulated public hearing are included on pages 50–52 of the student text and in Appendix B of this guide (pages 46–50).

E EVALUATION CRITERIA

The panel of evaluators may use the "Evaluator Guidelines for the Simulated Hearing" (Appendix E, pages 59–64) and the "Hearing Evaluation Rating Sheet," (Appendix F, pages 65–66) to help them through the hearing and rating process.

F | REFLECTION

As previously stated, Step 6 – "Reflecting on Your Learning Experience" deals with overall reflection on the Project Citizen process; however, it is important to conduct a reflection activity at the end of each step. This reflection should focus on the specific purpose and activities in that step. Some sample questions for reflection on Step 5 include the following:

1   How did you feel when you had to make your part of the presentation? Why did you feel that way?

2   Did your group work well together to present your section of the portfolio in the best way possible? Why or why not?

3   Did the audience you made your presentation to take you seriously and consider your policy recommendations? Why or why not?

4   What could your group have done differently to make a more effective presentation?

5   Has participating in Project Citizen made you more aware of the policymaking process in your community? Are you more or less likely to want to participate as a citizen in problem-solving in your community? Why?

TEACHING TIPS

Experienced teachers who have successfully taught Project Citizen to their classes shared the ideas and suggestions that follow.

1 Give students as much practice as possible in presenting their portfolio before they participate in a formal public presentation or appear before a government policymaking agency. Students may make a presentation for another class, school administrators and faculty, or former Project Citizen students. This also provides an opportunity for more students to make presentations and for students to gain added insight into their project.

2 Have students alternate the sections they present. For example, one student may present the alternative policies in front of another class and then present the action plan in front of the parent–teacher organization. This helps students understand the project as a whole.

3 Students may also assist each other in presentations. One student may point at graphs while another student describes them.

4 During the opening statement portion of an oral hearing, allow students to use note cards as a way of organizing their thoughts. Discourage them from reading directly from the cards.

5 While practicing for the hearings, use the opportunity to gain support for your students' policy by making presentations to groups who can then write letters of support. This step becomes part of the action plan.

6 When you practice your presentation, remember to practice answering sample evaluator questions. Also, on the day of the presentation, write on note cards some of the questions students have practiced and give them to evaluators ahead of time. It will help guide evaluators who may be inexperienced and will give your group familiar questions to answer.

7 Make every effort to arrange for the students to present their project before the appropriate policymaking body or agency.

8 When your students do have the opportunity to present their proposed policy before the appropriate policymaking body or agency, have them record their own reactions and reflections immediately after their presentation. Regardless of the outcome of the proceeding, it is important for students to realize that they might not get what they want the first time around. Students should understand that it does not mean they lost just because they may not have accomplished what they proposed.

STEP 6

REFLECTING ON YOUR LEARNING EXPERIENCE

PURPOSE

Discuss the purpose with students. The purpose of **Step 6** is to have students

- Think about and reflect on the project they have completed and their experience completing the project

- Learn how they might avoid mistakes in the future and improve their performance on other projects

Reflecting on the learning

When your class has completed its portfolio, a reflection section should be added to the documentation binder as a fifth section. It should feature students' answers to such questions as the following:

- What have you and your classmates learned?

- How did you and your classmates learn?

- What would you do differently if you were to develop another portfolio?

Reflecting on the learning experience should be a cooperative class effort similar to the class work conducted throughout this project. Students should be asked to record their reflections on their work as individuals, as well as their experiences as a small group and as a class. It may be helpful for the class to present its portfolio to an audience before developing this final section because questions and reactions from members of an audience provide important feedback.

Have students answer the questions under "Guidelines: Questions for Reflection" on pages 54-55 of the student book (see also Appendix G, pages 86–87). When that task is finished, engage in the following activity:

1   Lead a class discussion of student responses and try to arrive at several generalizations. Write them on a chalkboard or chart paper.

2   Divide the class into groups and assign each group one generalization. Each group should refine the statement of the generalization and provide evidence to support it.

3   The work of each group should then be given to a small writing team responsible for editing the work and preparing a draft for inclusion in the documentation section of the portfolio.

4   The entire class should review the draft created by the writing team and make suggestions for improvement.

5   The writing team should complete the draft for inclusion in the portfolio.

TEACHING TIPS

Experienced teachers who have successfully taught Project Citizen to their classes shared the ideas and suggestions that follow.

1 In addition to their individual reflections, have students take a reflection sheet home to their families. Ask students to engage in a discussion with their families regarding what they have learned from Project Citizen. The whole family can then answer the questions in the reflection sheet.

2 Invite the adults who worked with your students on the project to reflect with the class on their observations and their own experiences. Include the adult volunteers, community resource people who provided interviews or information, public officials with whom students met, and any other school personnel who took part.

APPENDICES

1   Suggestions for helping students

Assisting with tasks and procedures

Help students understand the steps they must take in developing their Project Citizen portfolios. When necessary, explain the tasks associated with developing the class portfolio and preparing for the simulated hearing. Review the Project Citizen Portfolio Criteria Checklist on page 49 of the student book and assist them in using it to perform a self-assessment of their completed work.

Gathering information

Help students identify sources of information that could be useful to them. Explain how to gather information about the problem under consideration efficiently and effectively. For example, you might help students

- Find information at the library

- Locate and use computers to find appropriate information or valuable resources available on the Internet

- Use telephone books or computer-based directories to locate government officials or agencies and appropriate private organizations that may provide pertinent information

- Contact people in the community who might be good sources of information

- Write letters or emails requesting information

- Prepare to interview resource individuals by role-playing that person

- Provide transportation to interviews and other places where they can find information

Preparing presentations

Coach students in creating and organizing oral presentations of their portfolio. Help set up presentations before community groups or government bodies.

Reflecting on the experience

Help students prepare written statements about what they have learned by participating in the Project Citizen program. Focus attention on what knowledge they gained, what civic skills they developed, and how their attitudes and dispositions about their roles as citizens in a representative democracy changed. What problems did they encounter and what would they do differently if they were to develop another portfolio?

2 Limiting your assistance

Gathering information

Do not assist students by

- Collecting information for them
- Writing letters and emails or making phone calls for them
- Doing research that they should be doing on their own

Portfolio preparation

Do not assist students by

- Writing materials for them to include in the portfolio
- Preparing their presentation statements
- Creating illustrations or other graphic materials
- Selecting materials to include in the portfolio

Oral presentation preparation

Adults should not prepare presentations for students.

These guidelines and procedures represent an effort to provide a consistent structure for national implementation of Project Citizen showcase events. We have attempted to make these guidelines and procedures as clear, concise, and useful as possible. We believe that everyone who participates in the various showcase events staged at the local, state, and national levels will appreciate clearly defined guidelines and uniform procedures and criteria for rating the portfolios and simulated hearings.

1   Participation

A major objective of Project Citizen is to encourage the widest possible participation from a broad range of students in various types of settings, including classrooms and youth groups sponsored by community organizations. For the purposes of the showcase events sponsored by the Center for Civic Education's network of Project Citizen coordinators, a class generally refers to all the students enrolled in a particular class or all the members of a youth group. It is expected that the majority of students involved in the class or youth group will be in the equivalent of grades five through eight, or approximately ten to fourteen years old.

2   Showcase events

There are two types of events that comprise a showcase. Both of these events involve adult members of the community rating the students' level of achievement using the guidelines and rating instruments provided in this guide.

A Portfolio display and evaluation

This event involves adult members of the community in reading, analyzing, and evaluating the portfolios produced by the students in a class or youth group. Typically, the portfolios are displayed in a prominent public venue and the rating takes place without students being present.

B Simulated hearing

This event involves all the students or youth group members who developed the portfolio. Each of the four groups of students who worked on the four sections of the portfolio are given an opportunity to make oral presentations and respond to follow-up questions from a panel of adult community members.

SHOWCASE PROCEDURE

1 Portfolio

The portfolio consists of two major components—
a four-panel display and a documentation binder.

The display consists of the following items:

- Four display panels of poster board, foam-core board, or the equivalent with each panel being no larger than 32 inches wide by 40 inches high; each of four portfolio groups in the class will have one panel to display its work; each panel should include

  - ▸ A written summary of the required topics

  - ▸ A variety of graphic illustrations

  - ▸ An identification of the sources used to gather information

The documentation binder consists of the following items:

- Five sections placed in a single three-ring binder no larger than 2 inches thick; each section should be separated by a divider and labeled on the tab

- An overall table of contents and a table of contents for each section

- Copies of important information each group has gathered for their section that best documents or gives evidence of their research

- A fifth section that contains the class's evaluation and reflection on their experience

2 Simulated hearing

Oral presentations by the participating students, in the form of a simulated hearing, are such an essential part of the Project Citizen learning experience that teachers are encouraged to include a simulated hearing before a panel of adult community members. These oral presentations can be made to other classes, parents, and adults, or to community groups such as the PTA, Rotary Club, etc. This activity will provide students with valuable experience in presenting ideas to others and in convincing an audience of a position to take on a vital public policy issue. Step 5 – "Presenting Your Portfolio," on pages 50–52 of the student book, outlines the goals and procedures for the class to use when making the oral presentations.

- In developing its portfolio and preparing for the simulated hearing, each class, or members of a youth group, is divided into four portfolio groups, one for each section of the portfolio.

- Each of the four portfolio groups will present a prepared four-minute statement about its research on the problem it studied. Students will then have six minutes to respond to follow-up questions from the panel of adult community members.

- An adult serving as a timer will indicate to students when one minute remains in the prepared testimony and again when one minute remains in the follow-up questioning.

- Students may use written notes for the four-minute prepared testimony but not for the follow-up questioning period.

- Students may refer to their portfolio display to emphasize a point at any time during either part of the oral presentation.

Timers

For each simulated hearing showcase, there should be an adult who serves as a timer. He or she should not be one of the panel members who will be rating the students' oral presentations. The timer should keep strictly to the ten-minute framework for each portfolio group presentation: four minutes for prepared testimony and six minutes for follow-up questioning. Timers will notify the students of the time remaining by holding up a card when they have one minute left in the prepared statement time and again when there is one minute left in the follow-up questioning period. When the full ten minutes has expired, the timer will stop the presentation by announcing "Time!"

3 Selecting evaluators

The following points will be helpful as you undertake the task of selecting adult members of the community to serve as evaluators to rate the students' level of achievement on their portfolios and in the simulated hearing:

- For every three portfolios in the showcase event, there should be a panel of three adults who will rate the students' achievement.

- These panels should be made up of individuals who are knowledgeable about the policymaking process, current public policy issues, and the link between civic education and civic participation.

- Evaluators should include prominent and knowledgeable community members from both the public and private sectors. A wide variety of individuals would be qualified to serve as evaluators. Think about inviting

  ▶ Active and retired teachers

  ▶ College professors

  ▶ Elected and appointed public officials

  ▶ Journalists

  ▶ Lawyers, judges, and law enforcement personnel

- ► Members of community organizations (League of Women Voters, Kiwanis Club, Veterans of Foreign Wars)

- ► High school students who have participated in the Center for Civic Education's We the People: The Citizen and the Constitution congressional hearing program

4 Materials

You will need to provide each evaluator with a copy of the Project Citizen textbook and photocopies of the following materials:

- • "Evaluator Guidelines for the Portfolio Showcase" (Appendix C, pages 51–56)

- • "Project Citizen Portfolio Evaluation Rating Sheet" (Appendix D, pages 57–58)

If the students are making oral presentations, the evaluators will need the following materials:

- • "Evaluator Guidelines for the Simulated Hearing" (Appendix E, pages 59–64)

- • "Project CItizen Hearing Evaluation Rating Sheet" (Appendix F, pages 65–66)

5 Evaluation

Conduct a briefing meeting with the individuals who will serve as evaluators of the students' work. Carefully review the overall goals of Project Citizen. Pay particular attention to the nature of middle school students and the expectations that evaluators should reasonably have for them.

Review each of the following with the portfolio evaluators:

- • "Evaluator Guidelines for the Portfolio Showcase" (Appendix C, pages 51–56)

- • "Project Citizen Portfolio Evaluation Rating Sheet" (Appendix D, pages 57–58)

If students will be making oral presentations,
review each of the following with the hearing evaluators:

- • "Evaluator Guidelines for the Simulated Hearing" (Appendix E, pages 59–64)

- • "Project Citizen Hearing Evaluation Rating Sheet" (Appendix F, pages 65–66)

Emphasize that evaluators need to give students some positive feedback. They should offer some constructive suggestions on how the students might improve their portfolio and their oral presentations.

As a general guideline, you will need one panel of three evaluators for every three portfolios being evaluated. Each portfolio will take approximately forty-five minutes to thoroughly review and rate. Each oral presentation will take approximately one hour.

For example, if there are fifteen portfolios to be evaluated, you will need at least five panels of three evaluators—fifteen ratings total. Each panel of evaluators would rate three different portfolios or three different oral presentations.

If possible, have each portfolio evaluated by two different panels of evaluators (six different individuals). And, if possible, have two different panels hear each simulated hearing presentation.

Collect all the judges' rating sheets at the conclusion of the portfolio or hearing evaluation. To determine the level of achievement for each portfolio or simulated hearing, combine all the individual evaluators' ratings and divide by the number of individual evaluators. The result is the average rating.

This average rating will give you a number you can use for determining different levels of achievement for the classes participating in the portfolio showcase or simulated hearing. The Center for Civic Education recommends the following rating ranges for determining the level of achievement:

Level of Achievement	Average Rating
Superior	41 – 50
Exceptional	31 – 40
Outstanding	21 – 30
Honorable Mention	0 – 20

EXAMPLE

Evaluator 1	38 total points
Evaluator 2	36 total points
Evaluator 3	40 total points
	114 total points

114 ÷ 3 = 38 (Exceptional)

6 After the evaluations

Hold an assembly of all participants, their teachers, families, and friends. Notify them of the showcase results.

- Give each participating student a Certificate of Achievement with his or her name on it and have it signed by a school administrator or elected public official. Your Project Citizen congressional district coordinator can obtain these certificates for you from the Center for Civic Education.

- If possible, arrange for a small trophy or plaque showing the level of achievement attained for each class that participated.

- If possible, arrange for a prominent community leader to present the Certificates of Achievement and give a brief address about the importance of citizens' engaging in the public policymaking process in their communities.

Evaluator Guidelines for the Portfolio Showcase

The Project Citizen portfolio showcase is the culmination of an interactive civic education program designed to actively engage adolescents in the civic life of their communities. In Project Citizen, the group of participating young people identify and analyze issues and problems facing their community (school, neighborhood, town, city, or state). As a group, students select one of these issues or problems for detailed study. After students complete their research, they propose a public policy to deal with that issue or problem. Then, they develop an action plan detailing the steps to take to have their public policy proposal adopted by the appropriate governmental authorities. Finally, the class develops a portfolio based on their research.

To develop the Project Citizen portfolio, the students or members of a youth organization are subdivided into four groups, one group for each section of the portfolio. The primary responsibility of each group is shown below.

Portfolio Group 1	Explaining the problem
Portfolio Group 2	Examining alternative policies
Portfolio Group 3	Proposing a public policy
Portfolio Group 4	Developing an action plan

The following information has been prepared to assist you in evaluating each of the components of the portfolio. The portfolio has two components: display and documentation. The two components taken together constitute the portfolio you will evaluate. For this purpose, you will use the "Project Citizen Portfolio Evaluation Rating Sheet" (Appendix D, pages 57–58). The "Project Citizen Portfolio Evaluation Rating Sheet" has five parts: four parts list the evaluation criteria for each section of the portfolio and one part gives the criteria for an overall evaluation of the students' work.

The following information corresponds to the four major sections that comprise the display component and the documentation binder.

Display section

The first display section should provide a detailed explanation of the issue or problem chosen and why the class selected it. A one- to two-page written summary should include a clear description of the issue or problem and what the class learned about it. Relevant graphs, photos, illustrations, or cartoons should be included. The students should cite all sources they used.

The written summary should be posted on the display and should include the following information:

- A clear statement of the nature of the issue or problem the students chose to research

- The degree of seriousness and scope of the issue or problem

- The levels of government or the government agencies that have responsibility for handling the issue or problem

- An indication of individuals or groups that might share responsibility for dealing with the issue or problem

- An indication of disagreements about the issue or problem in the community

- Whether there is an existing policy to deal with the problem

- If a policy exists, an explanation of its adequacy

Documentation binder

In the first section of the binder, the students must document their research, including a selection of the best supporting material. In addition to a table of contents, this section should include evidence that supports the group's work. Examples might include the following items:

- A completed "Problem Identification and Analysis Form" (Appendix G, page 68)

- A summary of the completed interview forms (or representative examples)

- Relevant newspaper or magazine articles

- Completed radio, television, Internet, or printed source forms (if applicable)

- Other relevant supporting articles, reports, etc.

Display section

The second display section should provide a detailed explanation and evaluation of two or three alternative public policy proposals from various groups or individuals. If an existing policy is in place, it should be included with an explanation of its effectiveness. Relevant graphs, photos, illustrations, or cartoons should be included. The students should cite all sources they used.

The display should include a one-page written summary for each alternative public policy presented. Each summary should include the following information:

- An explanation of the current public policy, if one exists, and an evaluation of its effectiveness (advantages and disadvantages)

- A detailed explanation of an alternative public policy solution and its strengths and weaknesses (advantages and disadvantages) with supporting data

- Identification of the source of the proposed public policy (e.g., individual citizens, special interest groups, legislature, or city council)

Documentation binder

In the second section of the documentation binder, the students must document their research, including a selection of the best supporting material. In addition to a table of contents, this section should include evidence that supports the group's work. Examples might include the following items:

- A copy of the full text of the policy (if one is currently in place)

- Letters or memos from special interest groups or individuals

- Publicity material circulating in the community

- Other relevant supporting articles, reports, etc.

Display section

The third display section should clearly explain a specific public policy proposal to address the issue or problem and the reasons that the class has agreed to support it. The class may choose to support an existing policy, modify an existing policy, create a new policy, or support one of the alternative policies described in the second display panel. Graphs, photos, illustrations, or cartoons should be displayed. The students should cite all sources used.

The display should contain a one- to two-page written summary that includes the following:

- An explanation of the public policy the class is proposing and a justification for how that public policy will best deal with the issue or problem

- The advantages and disadvantages of the public policy, supported with current data, including identification of individuals or groups that may be affected by it and a description of its possible impact

- A rationale statement that also identifies the appropriate branch of government or agency that would be responsible for implementing the proposed public policy

- An opinion statement on why the proposed public policy does not violate the U.S. Constitution or state constitutions

Documentation binder

In the third section of the documentation binder, the students must document their research, including a selection of the best supporting material. In addition to a table of contents, this section should include evidence that supports the group's work. Examples might include the following items:

- A completed copy of the "Constitutional Opinion Form" (Appendix G, page 83–84)

- Any laws, regulations, or rules that may apply

- A copy of an existing policy or law, or models of new or modified policies or laws

- Other relevant supporting articles, reports, etc.

Display section

The fourth display section of the portfolio should provide a detailed description of the process necessary to get the proposed public policy adopted and implemented by the appropriate government branch or agency. The plan should include steps for developing community support for the proposed policy. There should also be a detailed plan for overall implementation of the proposed public policy. Graphs, photos, illustrations, or cartoons should be displayed. The students should cite all sources they used.

The following information should be included in the written summary:

- A clear explanation of how the class would seek to gain support from government officials for the proposed public policy

- A clear explanation of how the class would seek to gain support from special interest groups, community groups, businesses, or influential individuals for the proposed public policy and action plan

- Identification of influential individuals, businesses, special interest groups, or government agencies that might speak out against the proposed public policy and action plan and an explanation of their opposition

- An explanation of the steps to be taken to implement the action plan and the plan's benefits

- Estimated costs and a timeline for implementation of the action plan, if possible

Documentation binder

In the fourth section of the documentation binder, the students must document their research, including a selection of the best supporting material. In addition to a table of contents, this section should include evidence that supports the group's work. Examples might include the following items:

- Written statements of support or opposition

- Publicity material

- Letters from influential individuals or public officials

- Other relevant supporting articles, reports, etc.

REFLECTIONS

This component is included only in the documentation binder. The final step of the Project Citizen curriculum asks students to reflect on their learning experience.

The fifth section of the documentation binder should contain brief statements or letters from students describing what they learned from Project Citizen. This should include reflection on what they learned about public policy and the policymaking process. It should explain how Project Citizen helped them to better understand the role of government officials and citizens. Finally, the reflection should address how they would approach the project differently if they did it again.

If the students have had an opportunity to present their portfolio to an audience in a simulated public hearing, they should include this experience in the reflection.

A Project Citizen portfolio consists of two components: a four-panel display and a five-section documentation binder. When evaluating the portfolio, the criteria on the next page should be applied to both the display and the corresponding section in the documentation binder.

Use the rating scale below to evaluate the portfolio. Give only one whole numeric rating (1–10) for each of the five sections of the Criteria for Evaluation.

Level of Achievement	Average Rating
Excellent	9 – 10
Above Average	7 – 8
Average	5 – 6
Below Average	3 – 4
Insufficient	1 – 2

PROJECT CITIZEN PORTFOLIO EVALUATION RATING SHEET

	EVALUATOR ▶		
	TEACHER ▶		
	SCHOOL NAME ▶		
SECTION	**CRITERIA FOR EVALUATION**	**RATING**	**COMMENTS**
1	**Understanding of the Problem** • States and explains the problem and its causes and presents evidence that there is a problem • Demonstrates an understanding of issues involved in the problem • Demonstrates an understanding of existing or proposed public policies • Explains disagreements about the problem that may exist in the community • Explains why government should be involved in the solution • Presents mutually supporting information in the display and binder		
2	**Analysis of Alternative Policies** • Presents two or three alternative public policies to address the problem • Explains advantages and disadvantages of each alternative policy presented • Identifies controversies and conflicts that may need to be addressed for each alternative • Presents mutually supporting information in the display and binder		
3	**Public Policy Development and Persuasiveness** • States a public policy that addresses the problem and identifies the governmental branch or agency responsible for enacting their proposed public policy • Supports the proposed public policy with reasoning and evidence • Identifies and explains advantages and disadvantages of the proposed public policy • Explains and supports the reasons why the proposed public policy is constitutional • Presents mutually supporting information in the display and binder		
4	**Implementation of an Action Plan** • Identifies individuals and groups, both supporters and opponents, who will need to be influenced • Identifies government officials, both supporters and opponents, who will need to be influenced • Outlines and explains an action plan for getting the proposed public policy enacted • Proposes action that builds and expands on evidence presented in previous panels • Presents mutually supporting information in the display and binder		
OVERALL PORTFOLIO	**Overall Portfolio** • Presents material in the display and binder that is mutually supportive • Constructs a clear and convincing sequence from one panel or section to the next • Uses and documents research from multiple sources and provides appropriate notation for the sources and research evidence used • Uses standards of good writing • Uses relevant and appropriate graphics and written information • Is visually appealing • Includes evidence of student reflection that states what students have learned (this appears in **Section 5** of the documentation binder)		
	TOTAL POINTS AWARDED ▶		

The Project Citizen simulated hearing is the culmination of an interactive civic education program designed to engage adolescents in the civic life of their communities. In Project Citizen, a group of participating young people identify and analyze issues and problems facing their community (school, neighborhood, town/city, state). They select one of these issues or problems for detailed study. After they complete their research, they propose a public policy to deal with that issue or problem. Finally, they develop an action plan detailing the steps to take to have their public policy proposal adopted by the appropriate government authorities.

The purpose of the simulated hearing (the oral presentation component) is to teach students to present and defend reasoned opinions related to influencing public policy decision-making in their communities.

For the simulated hearing, students or youth organization members are subdivided into four groups, one group for each section of the portfolio. Each group has the following responsibility for the following primary task:

Portfolio Group 1	Explaining the problem
Portfolio Group 2	Examining alternative policies
Portfolio Group 3	Proposing a public policy
Portfolio Group 4	Developing an action plan

Each group will make a prepared four-minute presentation. The group will then respond for six minutes to follow-up questions posed by you and other members of the evaluator panel. Each of the four groups will address your panel for a total of ten minutes. At the conclusion of each presentation, you and the other panel members should provide constructive feedback (see the "Feedback" section on page 64 for details).

The following information has been prepared to assist you in asking follow-up questions to each of the four groups. Please remember that these questions are suggested only as a guide to help you elicit additional information or elaborate on information presented in the testimony.

The purpose of the follow-up period and guiding questions is to help you determine how much the students have learned about the problem they have investigated and the information-gathering and problem-solving processes they have used. The more you learn about what the students have studied and proposed, the better you will be able to evaluate their presentation.

The following information has been prepared to assist you in evaluating the presentations of each of the four portfolio groups. The entire class developed a portfolio based on their research. The portfolio has two components: a display component and a documentation component. The two components taken together constitute the portfolio. The prepared statements and answers to your follow-up questions will be based on the portfolio. You will evaluate the student presentation using the five sections of the "Project Citizen Hearing Evaluation Rating Sheet" (Appendix F, pages 65–66), one for each of the four display and binder sections and one that is an overall evaluation of the students' presentations.

PORTFOLIO GROUP 1   Explaining the Problem

Portfolio Group 1 should provide a detailed explanation of the issue or problem chosen by the class and why that particular issue or problem was selected. During the prepared testimony phase, the group should be able to provide a detailed description of the problem's scope and impact on the community.

Possible follow-up questions might include the following:

- How widespread is this issue or problem in your community?

- Is this an issue or problem that people in your community think is important? How do you know?

- What has public reaction to the issue or problem been?

- What sources of information did you use to research the issue or problem?

- What more did you learn about the issue or problem as a result of your research?

- What branch of government do you think should be dealing with the issue or problem? Why?

- Are there policies, regulations, ordinances, or rules in place now that address the issue or problem? Do you believe they are adequate to deal with the problem? Why or why not?

Portfolio Group 2 should focus on explaining present or alternative policies designed to solve the problem or address the issue. In some instances, no policy exists, so students are expected to develop public policy alternatives to address the problem.

Testimony should include strengths and weaknesses of existing or proposed policies. Where no policy exists, students should explain what alternative policy proposals may be pending or are being recommended by their classmates, community groups, special interest groups, formal boards, the legislature, or city councils. Advantages and disadvantages of each policy or proposal should be presented and discussed.

Possible follow-up questions might include the following:

- What sources did you use to locate existing or proposed policies?

- What more did you learn about the issue or problem after you examined alternative policies?

- If a public policy currently exists, why does it need to be changed?

- Which groups or individuals support the existing policy or proposed new policy and what are the reasons for their support?

- Which groups or individuals oppose changing the policy or proposed new policy and what are the reasons for their opposition?

- Were there other policies or solutions that you did not include in your portfolio or in your presentation? If so, what are they? Why did you exclude them?

Portfolio Group 3 should focus on the policy or solution being proposed by the class. The group's explanation should include a clear rationale for making changes to existing policy, eliminating existing policy, or implementing new policy. If appropriate, the students should present a cost analysis. The group must include an explanation of why its proposed policy does not violate the federal or state constitutions.

Possible follow-up questions might include the following:

- What branch or agency of government is the proposed policy directed toward? Why is it directed toward this branch or agency?

- Have you considered the total cost of implementing your policy? Why or why not? If you have, what is the total cost and what is included in the cost?

- Where would the funds come from? What resources besides money might be needed?

- Does the civil community or private sector (business) have any responsibility to correct the problem or assist in carrying out the proposed public policy?

Portfolio Group 4 should focus on giving a detailed explanation of the steps needed to have the proposed policy adopted by the appropriate government officials. Testimony should include a statement on how long it might realistically take to get the proposed policy adopted and implemented.

Possible follow-up questions might include the following:

- How could the groups or individuals who support your proposal help to influence or convince government officials to adopt your proposal?

- Are there other individuals or groups who might support your recommended solution or policy? Why would they support your recommended solution or policy?

- What individuals or groups oppose your recommended solution or policy? What are the reasons for their opposition?

- How would you respond to the arguments of the individuals or groups that are opposed to your policy?

- How long would it take to implement the proposal?

- What results would you expect if you carried out your action plan?

- What do you think might happen if your proposal were not adopted?

GENERAL QUESTIONS

If appropriate, these general questions might be asked of any of the four groups:

- How does the [legal or law case] you mentioned in your testimony support your position?

- What did you learn about the role of government officials by participating in Project Citizen?

- What did you learn about the issues or problems facing your community by participating in Project Citizen?

FEEDBACK

The simulated hearing component of Project Citizen is an extension of classroom learning. As such, it presents another opportunity for you to help students understand the complexity of the public policymaking process. After each group presents its section of the portfolio, you are expected to provide the students with feedback on their presentation. These remarks should be short but constructive. You should commend the students for their work and help them learn from the process.

Always begin with positive remarks and add helpful examples of how the students might improve their presentation. For example, you might say "I liked the way you explained the problem statement. I would suggest that you include more data on the number of people affected by this serious problem."

Students will undoubtedly make errors in their presentation. During the feedback session, please make any corrections in a tactful, sensitive, and diplomatic manner. For example, "Your presentation included an important reference to the Supreme Court's ruling in *New Jersey v. T.L.O.* That case relates to the Fourth Amendment's prohibition of unlawful search and seizure. Because your presentation focused on free speech, you might think about using the *Tinker v. Des Moines* case instead."

A Project Citizen hearing provides an opportunity for students to share in a public forum what they have learned about a community problem and how they are proposing to solve it through the public policymaking process. The presentation will be made by four different groups of students, each presenting a different aspect of the entire group's research and their recommendation for a public policy.

When evaluating each group, consider the Criteria for Evaluation (on the next page) for that group of students and then use the rating scale. Give only one whole numeric rating (1–10) for each of the five sections of the Criteria for Evaluation.

Level of Achievement	Average Rating
Excellent	9 – 10
Above Average	7 – 8
Average	5 – 6
Below Average	3 – 4
Insufficient	1 – 2

PROJECT CITIZEN HEARING EVALUATION RATING SHEET

	EVALUATOR ▶		
	TEACHER ▶		
	SCHOOL NAME ▶		

GROUP	CRITERIA FOR EVALUATION	RATING	COMMENTS
1	**Understanding of the Problem** • States and explains the problem and its causes and presents evidence that there is a problem • Demonstrates an understanding of issues involved in the problem • Demonstrates an understanding of existing or proposed public policies • Explains disagreements about the problem that may exist in the community • Explains why government should be involved in the solution		
2	**Analysis of Alternative Policies** • Presents two or three alternative public policies to address the problem • Explains advantages and disadvantages of each alternative policy presented • Identifies controversies and conflicts that need to be addressed for each alternative		
3	**Public Policy Development and Persuasiveness** • States a public policy that addresses the problem and identifies the government branch or agency responsible for enacting their proposed public policy • Supports their proposed public policy with reasoning and evidence • Identifies and explains advantages and disadvantages of their proposed public policy • Explains and supportsthe reasons why their proposed public policy is constitutional		
4	**Implementation of an Action Plan** • Identifies individuals and groups, both supporters and opponents, who will need to be influenced • Identifies government officials, both supporters and opponents, who will need to be influenced • Outlines and explains an action process for getting their proposed public policy enacted • Proposes action that builds and expands on evidence presented in previous panels		
OVERALL HEARING	**Overall Hearing** • Constructs a clear and convincing sequence from one group to the next • Uses and documents research from multiple sources and makes reference to sources and research evidence used • References relevant and appropriate graphics and written information • Uses relevant and appropriate graphics and written information • Uses standards of good oral presentation (pace, projection, articulation, poise, eye contact) • Shares speaking responsibility while making the presentation • Includes evidence of reflection that states what the students learned		
	TOTAL POINTS AWARDED ▶		

The forms students need are in their textbooks in the appropriate places. To make the textbook usable with more than one class, we are providing photocopy masters of all student forms.

Discuss each form with students as they appear in the text and review with them how the forms are to be used to gather the information they will need. Provide them with a copy of each form as needed.

PROBLEM IDENTIFICATION AND ANALYSIS FORM

Names of group members _____

Date _____

The problem _____

1 Is this a problem that you and other people in your community think is important? Why?

_____

_____

2 What level of government or governmental agency is responsible for dealing with the problem?

_____

_____

3 What policy, if any, does government now have to deal with this problem?

_____

_____

If a policy does exist, answer the following questions:

- What are its advantages and disadvantages?

  _____

  _____

- How might it be improved?

  _____

  _____

- Does this policy need to be replaced? Why?

  _____

  _____

- What disagreements, if any, exist in your community about this policy?

  _____

  _____

  _____

4 Where can you get more information about this problem
   and the positions taken by different individuals and groups?

_____

_____

_____

5 Are there other problems in your community that you think
   might be useful for your class to study? What are they?

_____

_____

_____

_____

INTERVIEW FORM

Your name _____

Date _____

The problem _____

1   Name of person interviewed   _____

    Note: If a person does not wish to be named, respect his or her privacy and indicate only the person's role in the community (e.g., businessperson, retired person, parent, student, community volunteer).

2   Tell the person which problem you are studying. Then ask the following questions. Record the answers you receive.

    a   Is this a problem that you think is important? Why?

       _____

       _____

    b   Do you think others in our community believe this is an important problem? Why?

       _____

       _____

    c   What policy, if any, does government now have to deal with this problem?

       _____

       _____

    If a policy does exist, answer the following questions:

      •   What are the advantages of this policy?

        _____

        _____

      •   What are the disadvantages of this policy?

        _____

        _____

      •   How might the policy be improved?

        _____

        _____

      •   Does it need to be replaced? Why?

        _____

        _____

      •   What disagreements about this policy, if any, exist in our community?

        _____

        _____

    d   Where can I (or my class) get more information about this problem and the different positions people take on the problem?

       _____

       _____

PRINTED SOURCES FORM

Your name _____

Date _____

The problem _____

Name/date of publication _____

Title of the article _____

1   Position taken in the article related to problem
_____
_____

2   Main points of the position
_____
_____
_____
_____
_____

3   According to the source, what policy, if any, does government now have to deal with this problem?
_____
_____

If a policy does exist, answer the following questions:

* What are the advantages of this policy?
_____
_____

* What are the disadvantages of this policy?
_____
_____

* How might the policy be improved?
_____
_____
_____

* Does it need to be replaced? Why?
_____
_____
_____

* What disagreements about this policy, if any, exist in our community?
_____
_____
_____
_____

RADIO/TELEVISION/INTERNET SOURCES FORM

Your name _____

Date _____ Time_____

The problem _____

1 Source of information _____

   (This might be a website, television or radio news program, documentary,
   interview show, or some other program that addresses the problem.)

Consider the following questions as you gather information from your sources:

2 Is this a problem that is thought to be important? Why?

   _____
   _____
   _____

3 What policy, if any, does government now have to deal with this problem?

   _____
   _____
   _____

   If a policy does exist, answer the following questions:

   • What are the advantages of this policy?

      _____
      _____
      _____

   • What are the disadvantages of this policy?

      _____
      _____
      _____

   • How might the policy be improved?

      _____
      _____
      _____

   • Does it need to be replaced? Why?

      _____
      _____
      _____

   • What disagreements about this policy, if any, exist in our community?

      _____
      _____
      _____
      _____

INFORMATION FROM PRINT OR ELECTRONIC SOURCES FORM

Name(s) of research team member(s) _____

Date _____

The problem being researched _____

Name of library, office, agency, or website visited _____

1 Source of information
   a Name of publication/website _____
   b Author (if noted) _____
   c Date of publication/website _____

2 Record information from the publication or website that helps
   you answer as many of the following questions as you can.

   a How serious is this problem in our community?
      _____
      _____
      _____

   b How widespread is the problem in our state or nation?
      _____
      _____
      _____

   c Which of the following do you think is true?

      • There isn't a law or policy for dealing with the problem.   ❏ Yes ❏ No
      • The law for dealing with the problem is not adequate.   ❏ Yes ❏ No
      • The law for dealing with the problem is adequate,
        but it is not being well enforced.   ❏ Yes ❏ No

   d What levels of government or governmental agencies, if any, are responsible
      for dealing with the problem? What are they doing about the problem?
      _____
      _____
      _____
      _____

   e What disagreements about this policy or ways of dealing with it exist in our community?
      _____
      _____
      _____
      _____
      _____
      _____
      _____

INFORMATION FROM PRINT OR ELECTRONIC SOURCES FORM

f   Who are the major individuals, groups, or organizations expressing opinions on the problem?

_____

_____

_____

_____

_____

- Why are they interested in the problem?

  _____

  _____

  _____

  _____

  _____

- What positions are they taking?

  _____

  _____

  _____

  _____

  _____

- What are the advantages and disadvantages of their positions?

  _____

  _____

  _____

  _____

  _____

- How are they trying to influence government to adopt their position on the problem?

  _____

  _____

  _____

  _____

  _____

g   How can my classmates and I get more information on their positions?

_____

_____

_____

_____

_____

_____

DOCUMENTATION FORM
INFORMATION FROM LETTERS OR INTERVIEWS

Name(s) of research team member(s) _____

Date _____

The problem being researched _____

1 Source of information

   a Name _____

   b Title and organization _____

   c Address _____

   d Phone _____

2 Request information about the problem. After introducing yourself by letter or phone as suggested on page 22, ask for answers to the following questions:

   a How serious is this problem in our community?

   _____

   _____

   _____

   _____

   b How widespread is the problem in our state or nation?

   _____

   _____

   _____

   _____

   c Why is this a problem that should be handled by government? Should anyone else also take responsibility for solving the problem? Why?

   _____

   _____

   _____

   d Which of the following do you think is true?

      • There is no a law or policy for dealing with the problem.   ❏ Yes ❏ No

      • The law for dealing with the problem is not adequate.   ❏ Yes ❏ No

      • The law for dealing with the problem is adequate, but it is not being well enforced.   ❏ Yes ❏ No

   e What levels of government or governmental agencies, if any, are responsible for dealing with the problem? What are they doing about the problem?

   _____

   _____

   _____

   _____

DOCUMENTATION FORM
INFORMATION FROM LETTERS OR INTERVIEWS (CONTINUED)

f   What disagreements about this policy or ways of dealing with it exist in our community?

_____
_____
_____
_____

g   Who are the major individuals, groups, or organizations expressing opinions on the problem?

_____
_____
_____
_____

- Why are they interested in the problem?

_____
_____
_____

- What positions are they taking?

_____
_____
_____

- What are the advantages and disadvantages of their positions?

_____
_____
_____

- How can we get information on their positions?

_____
_____
_____

- How are they trying to influence government to adopt their positions on the problem?

_____
_____
_____

h   If our class develops a policy to deal with this problem,
how might we influence our government to adopt our policy?

_____
_____
_____
_____
_____
_____
_____

ANALYZING AND EVALUATING YOUR INFORMATION

For each piece of information you find that you think will be useful in developing the class portfolio, provide the following information. Attach this information to the item.

1   Name/title of the material _____
    Author (if there is one) _____
    Source (where it comes from) _____
    Date _____

2   Write a brief summary of the important information related
    to your problem that you found in this material.

    _____
    _____
    _____
    _____
    _____
    _____
    _____
    _____
    _____

3   This material could be used as evidence for

Explaining the Problem

❑ Display Panel
❑ Documentation Section

Proposed Public Policy

❑ Display Panel
❑ Documentation Section

Alternative Policies

❑ Display Panel
❑ Documentation Section

Action Plan

❑ Display Panel
❑ Documentation Section

4   Give a brief explanation of your choices.

    _____
    _____
    _____
    _____
    _____
    _____
    _____
    _____
    _____
    _____
    _____

TASK ONE   EXPLAINING THE PROBLEM

The first thing you and your classmates will need to do is to clearly explain the problem you have chosen. You will need to explain why the problem is important, which individuals or groups in the community are interested in this problem, and which part of government has responsibility for dealing with it. To accomplish this, you will need to answer the following questions:

1   What is the problem that you and your classmates want to study?

_____
_____
_____
_____
_____
_____

2   How serious is this problem in your community?

_____
_____
_____
_____
_____

3   How widespread is this problem in your community?

_____
_____
_____
_____
_____

4   Why is it a problem that should be handled by government?

_____
_____
_____
_____
_____

5   Should anyone else in the community take responsibility for solving the problem?

_____
_____
_____
_____
_____

6   Is there an existing law or policy for dealing with the problem?

_____
_____
_____
_____

7 If there is a law or policy, is it adequate to solve the problem?

_____

_____

_____

_____

_____

8 What disagreements, if any, are there in your community about
this problem and the way it is being handled?

_____

_____

_____

_____

_____

9 Who are the individuals, groups, or organizations with an interest in the problem?

_____

_____

_____

_____

_____

10 For each individual, group, or organization you identify, answer the following questions.
Use a separate sheet of paper for your answers.

- What is their position on the problem?

- Why are they interested?

- What are the advantages of their position?

- What are the disadvantages of their position?

- How are they trying to influence government to adopt their view?

11 What level of government or government agency is responsible
for dealing with this problem? Why?

_____

_____

_____

_____

_____

12 What is the government doing about the problem?

_____

_____

_____

_____

TASK TWO   EXAMINING ALTERNATIVE POLICIES

You must identify several alternative policies for dealing with the problem you have chosen. These policies may include an existing policy or policies being proposed by individuals or groups in the community. You should also include your own original ideas for policies to address the problem.

For each policy presented, you should

1   State the policy or suggested policy.

2   Identify the individual or group that is proposing the policy
    (this could be your own class or group).

3   Identify the advantages of this proposed policy.

4   Identify the disadvantages of this proposed policy.

5   Identify other individuals or groups in the community who are likely to support this policy.

6   Identify other individuals or groups in the community who are likely to oppose this policy.

Use the bottom of this page to write your answers for each policy you identify.
Use additional pages if necessary.

_____
_____
_____
_____
_____
_____
_____
_____
_____
_____
_____
_____
_____
_____
_____
_____
_____
_____
_____
_____
_____
_____

TASK THREE   PROPOSING A PUBLIC POLICY

Next, you will need to propose a public policy to deal with the problem. It must not violate the U.S. Constitution or your state's constitution. It may be one of the alternative policies you discussed earlier, a modification of one of those policies, or it may be your own original idea. Answer the questions below and complete the Constitutional Opinion Form on pages 44–45.

1   We think the best public policy to deal with this problem is

_____

_____

_____

_____

_____

_____

2   The advantages of this policy are

_____

_____

_____

_____

_____

_____

3   The disadvantages of this policy are

_____

_____

_____

_____

_____

_____

4   Identify the level of government that would be responsible for carrying out your proposed policy. Explain why this level of government is responsible.

_____

_____

_____

_____

5   The policy being proposed is constitutional because (use your answers from the Constitutional Opinion Form to complete this item)

_____

_____

_____

_____

_____

TASK FOUR DEVELOPING AN ACTION PLAN

You will need to develop an action plan to get your policy adopted by the appropriate governmental body or agency. This plan should include the steps you will need to take to get your proposed policy enacted and implemented by the government.

1   The main activities of our plan are

_____

_____

_____

_____

_____

_____

_____

_____

_____

2   Influential individuals and groups who might be willing to support our proposed policy are

_____

_____

_____

_____

_____

_____

_____

3   To win their support we can

_____

_____

_____

_____

_____

_____

_____

_____

4   Influential individuals and groups who might oppose our proposed policy are

_____

_____

_____

_____

_____

_____

_____

5   We might be able to win some support from these individuals and groups by

_____

_____

_____

_____

_____

_____

6   Influential government officials or agencies that
    might be willing to support our proposed policy are

_____

_____

_____

_____

_____

_____

_____

7   We can gain their support by

_____

_____

_____

_____

_____

_____

_____

8   Influential government officials or agencies that might oppose our policy are

_____

_____

_____

_____

_____

_____

9   We might be able to gain their support by

_____

_____

_____

_____

_____

CONSTITUTIONAL OPINION FORM

The United States Constitution and Bill of Rights place limits on what government can do in order to protect the rights of the people. So do the constitutions of each state.

Whenever we suggest that government adopt a policy or enact a law to deal with a problem, it is important that we do not ask government to do something prohibited by our federal or state constitutions. Each citizen has the right and should take the responsibility to look at present and suggested policies and laws to see if they might be violating constitutional limits on government.

This checklist includes some of the most important limits our federal and state constitutions place on our governments to protect our rights. Use the checklist when you develop your policy. Be sure that, in your opinion, your proposed policy does not violate the limits placed on government.

This Constitutional Opinion Form should be considered by the entire class. The results of this consideration should be included in Part 3 of the display and documentation sections of your portfolio.

Checklist

1 Government is not allowed to interfere with a person's freedom of belief. Our proposed policy (does/does not) violate this limit on the power of government. Explain why.

_____

_____

_____

_____

_____

_____

2 Government is not allowed to place unreasonable and unfair limits on a person's right to express himself or herself in speech, writing, or by other means. Our proposed policy (does/does not) violate this limit on the power of government. Explain why.

_____

_____

_____

_____

_____

_____

3 Government is not allowed to take a person's life, liberty, or property without giving that person a fair hearing in a court of law or before another authorized agency of government. Our proposed policy (does/does not) violate this limit on the power of government. Explain why.

_____

_____

_____

_____

_____

_____

4 Government is not allowed to invade the privacy of a person's home without a very good reason for doing so. Our proposed policy (does/does not) violate this limit on the power of government. Explain why.

_____
_____
_____
_____
_____
_____

5 Government is not allowed to make laws that unreasonably or unfairly discriminate against people on the basis of race, religion, age, ethnic group (national origin), or gender. Our proposed policy (does/does not) violate this limit on the power of government. Explain why.

_____
_____
_____
_____
_____
_____

Summary Statement

Write a summary statement in which you support your belief that your class's proposed public policy does not violate the U.S. Constitution or your state's constitution.

_____
_____
_____
_____
_____
_____
_____
_____
_____
_____
_____
_____
_____
_____
_____
_____
_____
_____
_____

PROJECT CITIZEN PORTFOLIO CRITERIA CHECKLIST

As you and your classmates complete your portfolio and prepare for the hearing, it is important to check your work to make sure you have included everything. This checklist will help you to determine whether you have met the criteria that evaluators will use to rate your work.

TASK	CRITERIA FOR EVALUATION	YES	NO	NEEDS WORK
1	**Understanding of the Problem**			
	• States and explains the problem and its causes and presents evidence that there is a problem			
	• Demonstrates an understanding of issues involved in the problem			
	• Demonstrates an understanding of existing or proposed public policies			
	• Explains disagreements about the problem that may exist in the community			
	• Explains why government should be involved in the solution			
	• Presents mutually supporting information in the display and binder			
2	**Analysis of Alternative Policies**			
	• Presents two or three alternative public policies to address the problem			
	• Explains advantages and disadvantages of each alternative policy presented			
	• Identifies controversies and conflicts that may need to be addressed for each alternative			
	• Presents mutually supporting information in the display and binder			
3	**Public Policy Development and Persuasiveness**			
	• States a public policy that addresses the problem and identifies the governmental branch or agency responsible for enacting the proposed public policy			
	• Supports the proposed public policy with reasoning and evidence			
	• Identifies and explains advantages and disadvantages of the proposed public policy			
	• Explains and supports the reasons why the proposed public policy is constitutional			
	• Presents mutually supporting information in the display and binder			
4	**Implementation of an Action Plan**			
	• Identifies individuals and groups, both supporters and opponents, who will need to be influenced			
	• Identifies government officials, both supporters and opponents, who will need to be influenced			
	• Outlines and explains an action plan for getting the proposed public policy enacted			
	• Proposes action that builds and expands on evidence presented in previous panels			
	• Presents mutually supporting information in the display and binder			
OVERALL	**Overall Portfolio**			
	• Presents material in the display and binder that is mutually supportive			
	• Constructs a clear and convincing sequence from one panel or section to the next			
	• Uses and documents research from multiple sources and provides appropriate notation for the sources and research evidence used			
	• Uses standards of good writing			
	• Uses relevant and appropriate graphics and written information			
	• Is visually appealing			
	• Includes evidence of student reflection that states what students have learned (this appears in **Section 5** of the documentation binder only)			

You may use the following questions to reflect on what you have learned.

1   What did you learn about the
   - problems facing your school, neighborhood, town, or state?
   - meaning of public policy and the policymaking process?
   - responsibility and authority of government officials to help solve problems in the community?
   - role of the different branches of government and government agencies in your community or state?
   - role of citizens in helping to make public policy decisions that serve the needs of the community?

2   What other important things did you learn when you did Project Citizen?

3   What skills did you develop as you worked on your project?
   For example, what skills did you use for
   - gathering information?
   - finding solutions?
   - making decisions?
   - working with people?

4   What other skills did you use or learn?

5   What did you learn about what it takes to be a responsible citizen in a democracy? For example,
   - What do we mean by individual rights and why is it important to protect them?
   - Why is it important to be open-minded?
   - Why is it sometimes necessary to negotiate and compromise?
   - What do we mean by the general welfare and why do we need to promote it?

6   What rights and responsibilities of citizens did you exercise when you were fulfilling the tasks of Project Citizen?

7   What responsibilities of public officials did you learn about when you were fulfilling the tasks of Project Citizen?

8   What did you learn about democratic values and principles?

You may use the following questions to reflect on your experiences.

1   What did I learn about public policy from working with my classmates?

2   What did we learn as a class about public policy by developing our portfolio?

3   What skills did I acquire or improve by working on this project?

4   What skills did we acquire or improve by working on this project?

5   What are the advantages of working as a team?

6   What are the disadvantages of working as a team?

7   What did I do well?

8   What did we do well?

9   How can I improve my problem-solving skills?

10   How can we improve our problem-solving skills?

11   What would we want to do differently if we were to develop another portfolio on another public policy issue?

Additional useful items that do not appear in the student textbook are as follows:

My definition of public policy

Essential elements of public policy

My revised definition of public policy

STUDENT HANDOUT 2   WHAT IS AND WHAT IS NOT PUBLIC POLICY?

Read the first example of a community problem (shown in the middle column below) and the examples of a public policy solution to the problem by a government institution acting with or without civil society (left column) and a solution to the problem solely by civil society (right column). Then fill out the rest of the chart with your own suggestions for public policy and civil society solutions to the problems noted. Use the last space to identify a problem in your community and give examples of public policy and civil society solutions for it. After you have come up with your responses, share them with your group members or classmates.

PUBLIC POLICY SOLUTION	COMMUNITY PROBLEM	CIVIL SOCIETY SOLUTION
City officials fund a program to give needy individuals vouchers to "buy" food and clothing from participating merchants	Poor families in the community need food and adequate clothing	Members of a religious organization conduct a drive to collect food and clothing and then distribute the items to the needy
	School-aged children are out on the streets late at night	
	Parents are not using child protective car seats properly	
	The lake in the community is polluted and filled with litter	
	Owners of a professional football team want to build a stadium in the city	
	Many students in the local high school have been cheating on homework and tests	

© 2009 Center for Civic Education

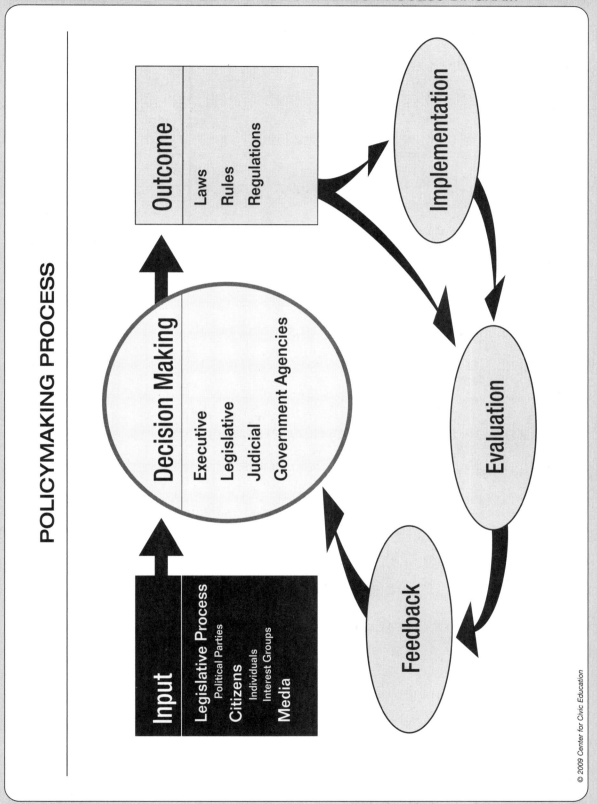

POLICYMAKING PROCESS

Input

Legislative Process
Political Parties

Citizens
Individuals
Interest Groups

Media

Decision Making

Executive
Legislative
Judicial
Government Agencies

Outcome

Laws
Rules
Regulations

Implementation

Evaluation

Feedback

A   BRANCHES AND LEVELS OF GOVERNMENT

DIRECTIONS

Fill in each of the three columns with the name of the person or office appropriate for each level of government. Add other levels of government in your area and complete the chart for them as well.

Level of Government	Executive	Judicial	Legislative
State	Governor		
Town or City			
Other (Level of Government)			
Other (Level of Government)			

B   RESPONSIBLE GOVERNMENT AGENCIES

DIRECTIONS

In the left column, write a short description of two or three of the public policy problems you identified in Activity B on page 5. Then, write the name of the responsible or authorized government official or agency in the column to the right.

	Public Policy Problem	Responsible or Authorized Government Official or Agency
Example	Traffic in front of our school	Santa Monica Police Department
1		
2		
3		

WHO ARE THE RESPONSIBLE POLICYMAKERS?

Issue or Problem   Many kids are skipping school

Policymakers

Principal	School Board	City Council	State Education Department	State Legislature

Possible Action

Start a counseling program for kids who skip school	Adopt a policy of minimum requirements for school attendance in order to pass	Direct police to work with school officials to return to class all students caught skipping	Require every school to have a procedure for dealing with kids who skip	Pass a law that fines parents whose kids skip school

© 2009 Center for Civic Education

WHO ARE THE RESPONSIBLE POLICYMAKERS?

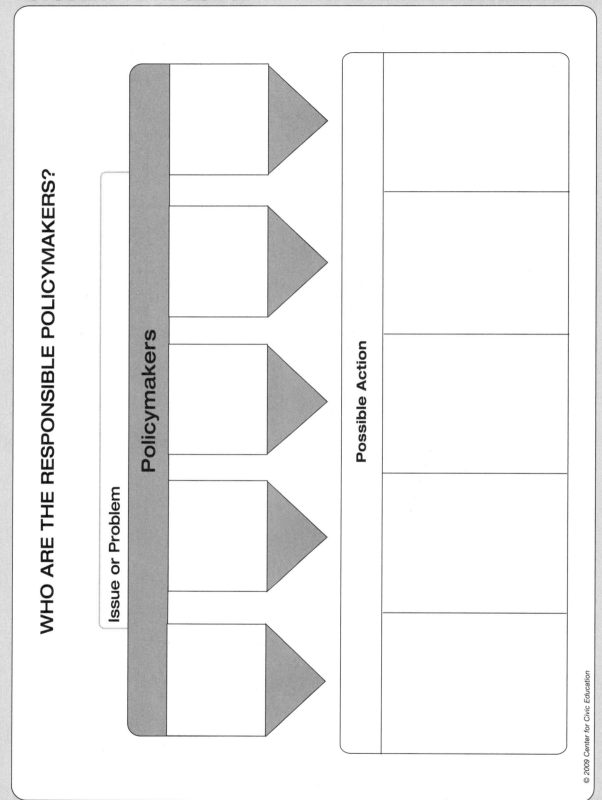

Issue or Problem

Policymakers

Possible Action

STUDENT HANDOUT 6   PROPOSING A PUBLIC POLICY

Writing the appropriate language for a public policy or a bill can be tricky. Sometimes even the people who serve as state legislators need help. The following guidelines are taken from the Montana State Legislature's website. It provides state legislators with a series of questions they need to answer so that the people in the bill-drafting office of the legislature can turn their ideas into a bill and then, if passed by the legislature, a law.

Review the ten questions that the legislators need to answer. They can help you as you prepare the class policy you need when you are working on the third task of the portfolio development—proposing a public policy. Although you may not be writing actual legislation for your policy, the questions will help you clarify your thinking about what you should be addressing.

When an employee of the Legislative Services division drafts a bill for a legislator, he or she must translate the objectives and policies of the legislator into clear, concise language that meets the requirements of the *Bill Drafting Manual*. To do this, the drafter needs complete information from the requesting legislator.

Legislative Council rules say that "All bill drafting requests must be specific as to what the legislator wishes to accomplish and must also outline the method which will achieve that end. A drafter, with the concurrence of the executive director (of Legislative Services), is authorized to return a bill drafting request to a legislator for more information."

A legislator requesting a bill should be able to answer as many of the following questions as possible.

1   What exactly is the problem that needs to be solved?

2   Who has experienced the problem? Is it perceived as widespread or local in nature?

3   What is the proposed solution to the problem?

4   How should the solution be achieved, i.e., what action should government take to intervene in the problem?

5   What results are desired? If the bill passes, what results would show that the solution had been achieved?

6   Who should the drafter contact for information? (Be sure to give a copy of this form to each person you name, indicating that they should be prepared to answer these questions.)

7   Do you know of specific existing statutes that need to be changed to achieve your proposed solution?

8   Is there specific legislation from another state, organization, lobbyist, agency, or other source that could serve as a model for your bill? If you think you heard or read about something somewhere, try to remember as specifically as possible where you learned of it. If you have a copy, please provide it.

9   Does the solution require additional money? How should the money be raised or from what existing source should it come? (Mandates to local governments must authorize a source of funding.)

10   What alternatives to legislation have been considered to solve the problem? How have they failed?

Source: http://leg.mt.gov/css/research/information/draftques.asp

Examples of class portfolios presented at the National Conference of State Legislatures' showcase.

CENTER FOR CIVIC EDUCATION PUBLICATIONS

Foundations of Democracy (Middle School)
Authority, Privacy, Responsibility, and Justice

The *Foundations of Democracy* series consists of curricular materials for students from kindergarten through twelfth grade on four concepts fundamental to an understanding of politics and government: Authority, Privacy, Responsibility, and Justice. This multidisciplinary curriculum draws upon such fields as political philosophy, political science, law, history, literature, and environmental studies. (Suggested grades 6–9)

Visit **http://www.civiced.org/metrics/pctg1**

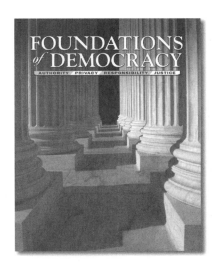

Project Citizen (Level 2)

Project Citizen (Level 2) is designed for use in high school and college-level courses, introducing students to the citizen's role in the public policy-making process. Project Citizen is designed to foster the development of students' interest and ability to participate competently and responsibly in local, state, and federal government. It can also be used with groups of adults who are interested in becoming more effectively involved in community affairs. (Suggested grades 9–12)

Visit **http://www.civiced.org/metrics/pctg1**

We the People: The Citizen & the Constitution (Middle School Level 2)

With more than 270 illustrations and images, the 2007 edition of *We the People: The Citizen & the Constitution* teaches the history and principles of constitutional democracy in the United States. The middle school curriculum, consisting of thirty lessons presented in six units, uses critical-thinking exercises, problem-solving activities, cooperative-learning practices, and a culminating performance assessment. The full-color, 352-page text is accompanied by a teacher's edition. (Suggested grades 7–9)

"The Level 2 *We the People* text represents civic education at its best. It engages students and allows them to participate in thoughtful, critical, and analytical discussions of the historical background and current issues facing our constitutional government."

Donna Paoletti Phillips
2006 American Civic Education
 Teacher Awards Recipient

Visit **http://www.civiced.org/metrics/pctg1**

Representative Democracy in America

Representative Democracy in America: Voices of the People is a six-part video series on DVD and VHS designed to help high school students understand our system of representative democracy. The six programs, each approximately fifteen minutes in length, address the following topics:

- The roots of representative democracy
- Federalism and the separation of powers
- The roles of representatives, executives, and justices in our democracy
- Our representatives and how they are chosen
- The role of the citizen in a representative democracy

The *Video Series Instructional Guide* includes twelve lesson plans, a synopsis of each program, a bibliography, and correlations to the *We the People: The Citizen & the Constitution* (Level 3) text. A printed copy of the instructional guide accompanies each DVD and VHS. A digital version of the instructional guide is also available on the DVD.

Visit **http://www.civiced.org/metrics/pctg1**

American Legacy

American Legacy: The United States Constitution and Other Essential Documents of American Democracy is an 80-page, pocket-sized (3.5″x 6.5″) booklet that includes the U.S. Constitution and the Declaration of Independence together with passages from twenty-seven other documents that encompass essential ideas of American democracy. The documents are arranged chronologically, beginning with the Mayflower Compact. Included are excerpts from such documents as *The Federalist*, Chief Justice John Marshall's decision in *Marbury v. Madison*, George Washington's Farewell Address, Thomas Jefferson's First Inaugural Address, Sojourner Truth's "Ain't I a Woman?", Abraham Lincoln's First Inaugural Address, the Gettysburg Address, the Emancipation Proclamation, Learned Hand's "The Spirit of Liberty," Martin Luther King Jr.'s "I Have a Dream" speech, and the Civil Rights Act of 1964. The booklet includes an extensive index to the Constitution.

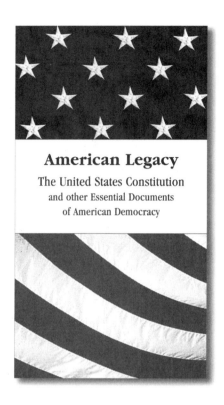

American Legacy
The United States Constitution
and other Essential Documents
of American Democracy

"*American Legacy* is an absolute necessity. I use every document in the book, but especially focus upon the Declaration of Independence, the Constitution, and the *Federalist Papers* to teach students the ideals of the United States."

Nathan Breen
Social Studies Teacher
Cheyenne Central High School
Cheyenne, Wyoming

Visit **http://www.civiced.org/metrics/pctg1**